WITHDRAWN
HIRAM COLLEGE LIBRARY

THE
MORNING WATCH

Books by James Agee

PERMIT ME VOYAGE

LET US NOW PRAISE FAMOUS MEN
(*with Walker Evans*)

THE MORNING WATCH

130121

THE
MORNING WATCH

by James Agee

HOUGHTON MIFFLIN COMPANY · BOSTON

The Riverside Press Cambridge

SECOND PRINTING   R

COPYRIGHT, 1950, BY JAMES AGEE

ALL RIGHTS RESERVED INCLUDING THE RIGHT
TO REPRODUCE THIS BOOK OR PARTS THEREOF IN ANY FORM

This story first appeared in Botteghe Oscure, *Rome*

PRINTED IN THE U.S.A.

THE
MORNING WATCH

❧ I ❧

4-71 direct Literall Roan 3.44

THE
MORNING WATCH

I

*My soul fleeth unto the Lord
before the morning watch: I say,
before the morning watch.*

— PSALM CXXX

IN HIDDEN VAINGLORY he had vowed that he would stay awake straight through the night, for he had wondered, and not without scorn, how they, grown men, could give way to sleep on this night of all the nights in their life, leaving Him without one friend in His worst hour; but some while before midnight, still unaware that he was so much as drowsy, he had fallen asleep; and now this listen-

3

ing sleep was broken and instantly Richard lay sharp awake, aware of his failure and of the night.

Too late: already it was time: now it was the deepest hour of the deepest night. Already while he slept, with wrathful torches and with swords and staves they had broken among the branches of the Garden; Judas, gliding, had stretched against that clear Face his serpent's smile; Peter in loyal rage had struck off the dazed servant's ear and He in quiet had healed him: and without struggle had yielded Himself into their hands. Could ye not watch with me one hour? No Lord, his humbled soul replied: not even one: and three times, silently, gazing straight upward into the darkness, he struck his breast while tears of contrition, of humility and of a hunger to be worthy, solaced his eyes, and awakened his heart. O yes it was an hour more deep by far than the Agony and Bloody Sweat: no longer alone, unsure; resolved, and taken. That was already fully begun which could come only to one ending. By now He stood peaceful before Pilate, the one calm and silence amid all that tumult of malice and scorn and guile and hatred and beating of unhabitual light through all the sleepless night of spring; while in the dark porchway, even at this moment, the servant girl persistently enquired of Peter and he in fury and in terror denied his Lord:

now the bitter terrible weeping and now, saluting this mortal morning, the cock's triumphal and reproaching cry. A deep, deep hour. Soon now the sentence and the torment, the scourging, the mocking robe, the wreathed, wretched Crown: King of the Jews.

O God, he silently prayed, in solemn and festal exaltation: make me to know Thy suffering this day. O make me to know Thy dear Son's suffering this day.

Within Thy Wounds hide me.

Suffer me not to be separated from Thee.

From the Malicious Enemy defend me.

By a habit of their own, meanwhile, his hands searched and tested along the undersheet, and now they told him that this time he had wet the bed so little that by morning nobody would know. He let out a long thankful breath and looked down along his bed.

All he could see at first throughout the long room was a kind of gelatin glimmer at the alcoved windows, and the aisled ends of the iron cots at right angles to his own: but when the foot which had awakened him lifted from the yielding board and it creaked again he saw in his mind's eye, large and close, the coarse-ribbed shambling stocking, flecked with lint, and knew that Father Whitman must be very tired; for to judge by the hissing sound, his feet scarcely left the floor. He wondered whether Father Whitman was sleeping at all, tonight.

Father Whitman touched a foot and whispered: "Quarter of four."

"Okay Fathuh," Hobe Gillum said in his clear hard voice.

"Quiet," Father Whitman said sharply.

"Okay Fathuh," Hobe whispered.

Now that the priest came nearer as silently as he could between the ends of the cots, Richard could see the tall ghostly moving of his white habit.

Father Whitman stopped at Jimmy Toole's cot, touched his foot, and whispered: "Quarter of four." Jimmy mumbled something in a light sad rapid voice and stuck his head under his pillow.

Father Whitman stepped between the cots and touched his shoulder. "Quarter of four," he whispered more loudly.

"Cut it out," Jimmy whined in his sleep.

Richard heard Hobe's knees hit the floor.

Father Whitman shook Jimmy's shoulder. "Quarter of —— "

"*Quit* it you *God damn* —— " Jimmy snarled, wrenching aside the pillow; then, with servile Irish charm: "Aw sure Father, I din know it was *you* Father."

At the far end of the dormitory there was a wild stifled snicker.

"Time to get up," Father Whitman whispered.

The snickering became happier and happier. Father Whitman spoke more loudly into the darkness: "Now cut that out fast or you'll be sorry you ever started it."

The snickering persisted as if uncontrollably, but now it was blunted in a pillow. Father Whitman ignored it. "Better get straight out of bed," he told Jimmy. "You'll go back to sleep."

Hobe was buttoning his shirt.

Without a word Jimmy rolled out of bed onto his knees and buried his head in his arms.

Now that Father Whitman came toward him, Richard shut his eyes. When he knew he was about to be touched he opened his eyes and whispered, "All right Father." He saw the stopped hand and, much nearer and larger than he had expected, the beaten, enduring horse face; he became aware of his deceitfulness and was ashamed of it.

"All right," Father Whitman said. Bet he says quarter of four, Richard thought. "Quarter of four," Father Whitman said.

"Yes Father."

"Put your shoes on downstairs," he whispered, and turned away. "Put your shoes on downstairs," he told Hobe, "and don't let Jimmy go to sleep again."

"Okay Fathuh," Hobe said, gallusing himself into his overalls.

"And don't you dawdle when you're done," Father Whitman told him. "You kids see to it you come right back here to bed."

"Yes suh Fathuh."

"Don't think I won't be watching for you."

"No suh Fathuh."

Richard knelt by his cot and sank his face in his hands. O God, he prayed, I thank Thee that I did not wet the bed this night — enough to get caught, he added carefully, remembering Thou God seest me; for Jesus' sake Amen.

He said swiftly to himself the prayer Father Weiler had taught them as enough when, for any good reason, you did not have time enough for more: I praise my God this day I give myself to God this day I ask God to help me this day Amen.

Gripping his hair and pressing the heels of his hands tightly against his closed eyes he tried as hard as he could to realize what was happening as he had in the moment of waking. But now he could realize only what a special night this was, what grave and holy hours these were. There seemed to be a strange stillness and power in the air as there always was on very special occasions and never at ordinary times; it made him feel dry, light of weight, very watchful, expectant and still, and it almost made his scalp tingle. It was something like the feeling of his birthday, and of Christmas, and of Easter, and it was still more like the feeling he now seldom and faintly recalled, during the morning just after he learned of his father's death, and during the day he was buried. But it was not really like any of these, or anything else, except itself. These were the hours of Our Lord's deepest Passion. For almost forty days now this feeling had grown and deepened, not without interruption, for he had not managed perfectly to keep either his public or his secret Lenten Rules; yet he had been sufficiently earnest and faithful, and sufficiently grieved in his failures, that the growth had been deeper and more cumulative and more rewarding than he had ever known before; and now he was coming into the heart of it, the holiest and most solemn of its shrines, with heart and soul prepared and eager. Already it was no longer Maundy Thursday, the birthday of the Eucharist; that sorrowfully jubilant magnificence was turned under the world; already the world was brought a few hours forward into the most gravely majestic of all days, Good Friday; already the wheel was so turned that high upon darkened heaven white Easter dazzled, suspended, the crown of the year, like the already trembling start of an avalanche. Easter was very soon now, so soon, with his throat brimming with its hymns and his soul ardent for release and celebration, that it was difficult to be patient; yet his faith and absorption were such that at the same time he came into this day as sorrowing and careful as if Christ had never been crucified before, and could never rise from the dead. Yet now that he desired to retrieve his waking awareness he could not, but only knelt, sad, trying to taste the peculiar quality of the night and to distinguish it from other auras of momentousness, until, realizing how he had misled himself, he gripped his hair and pressed his eyeballs the more tightly, repeating in his heart: Jesus our Lord is crucified. Jesus our Lord is crucified. He saw the Head.

Thrown with fury, a shoe struck the wall next Jimmy's bed: the noise broke upon Richard with sickening fright. Then Hobe's voice:

"All right some mothuf ----- sonofabitch is agoana git the livin s - - t beat outn him if I find out who throwed that!"

"Shet yer God damn mouf," said a coldly intense, deeper voice at the far end of the dormitory.

"Yeah fer Chrise sakes *shut up*," said another voice, as several neutral voices said "Shut up."

In the rigid silence Richard and Jimmy dressed quickly while Hobe waited. Carrying their shoes they stole barefoot on tiptoe from the room and along the hall and past the iron cot which had been set up by the stairhead for this one night for Father Whitman. They could just make out how he lay there in the dark in his long white habit, giving off a current of silent and ominous power because they could not be sure as they passed whether he was asleep or aware of them; the clacking of his tin clock filled the pine stairwell with its flagrant loudness. They tried hard not to creak the stairs. The pit of Richard's stomach still felt as it did when, without being too mad or too desperate to care, he knew it was impossible not to fight. By trying hard he was able to restore whole to his mind the thorn-crowned image of his Lord, but now it was not as he had seen it in prayer beside his cot but was very little different from a pious painting he knew: the eyes rolled up in a way that seemed affected, and in his cold sickness the image meant little to him. It was not until they came onto the back porch that the open night put them once more at their ease.

"Sonofabitchin mothuf - - - - - bastud," Hobe said. "At shoe bettah be gone by mawnin or *some* bastudly cocks - - - - - 's agoana be sorry."

"Aw shut up Hobie," Jimmy said. "This ain't no time to talk like that."

"Hell do *I* keer," Hobe said. "*I* hain't been to Confession yet."

But he started on down the steps without saying anything more.

"What happened?" Richard asked.

"Jis trine wake up Jimmy," Hobe said. "God All Mighty Christ, can't even wake nobody up in this friggin School — "

Richard followed them down the steps. He was glad he had learned hardly even to think of saying anything. If Jimmy told Hobie to shut up and quit cussing Hobie would take it off of him, they were buddies; but by now he knew enough to keep *his* mouth shut. He felt uneasy, though, because he was glad he had not sworn. That was like being thankful you were not as other men and that was one of the worst sins of all; the Pharisee.

He had forgotten all about the shoes he carried and now that unexpectedly, for the first time this year. he felt the ground against the bare soles of his feet it was as if, fumbling among clothes in a dark closet, he had put his hand on living flesh. Even though the ground in this schoolyard was skimmed with dusty gravel, its aliveness soared through him like a sob and lifted his eyes in wonder upon the night. There was no moon and what few stars were out, they were made faint by a kind of smiling universal milky silence, not fog, or even the lightest kind of mist, but as if the whole air and sky were one mild supernal breath. Downhill in the Chapel a line of small windows meekly smoldered, dark orange; he followed his companions and saw that they too were carrying their shoes. When they came to the lawn beyond their building they left the gravel; the ground, with its scarce new grass, felt like a fish. There was a thick oak near the center of the lawn and Hobe and Jimmy, as they passed, stung it several times expertly with gravel. It had not occurred to Richard to pick up gravel and now he was glad, for he was sure he would have missed as often as hit.

THE
MORNING WATCH

II

THE
MORNING WATCH

II

THE NIGHT SMELLED like new milk; the air which exhaled upon them when they opened the side door of the Chapel was as numb and remote as the air of a cave. Without knowing it they hesitated, subdued by the stagnant darkness and its smell of waxed pine and spent incense. Across the unlighted nave the open door of the Lady Chapel brimmed with shaken light; but just at their left, through the door to

17

the vestry, came a friendlier and more mundane light, a delicious smell, and the tired grinding of the voice they most admired in the world. When he became aware of their hesitation beside this partly closed door, George Fitzgerald spoke to them with a formality as unaccustomed and gentle as if a dead body lay in the room behind him and they came in, silent and shy. By the loud hurrying little clock it was still only four minutes to four. They squatted on their bare heels against the wall and looked on, their six eyes emphatic in the sleepless light.

The inward wall of this long corridor was hung solid with cassocks and they were of all lengths from a size almost big enough for the giant sad boy they all called Undertaker, to the all but baby size of Dillon Prince. At first Richard wondered where all the cottas were; in the laundry for Easter, he realized. The room was so weakly lighted by candlestubs that at the far end it was hardly possible to dintinguish the red cassocks from the black. Just within the surer light, his jaw and his shoulders sloping more heavily even than usual with fatigue and with his low posture, Willard Rivenburg sat on a folding-chair which gave out dangerous splintering noises whenever he stirred. It was he who was talking, aimlessly, quietly, almost in his sleep; and Richard could see that

George and Lee Allen answered him only so often as courtesy required, never turning their attention from their work. Not only were they Prefects; it was also believed by some of the older people that they alone among the boys now at the School, might have a Vocation. They were in their last year now and it was generally understood that they were both praying hard for this to be made clear to them before they graduated. It was their privilege, tonight, to trim and change the candles and to remove and replace the withering flowers, and now white-girdled, incongruous in red cassocks, they stood wearily beside a soup plate, replying gravely in short words while, their eyes bright with the lateness of the hour and fixed in the profound attentiveness of great scientists, they revolved candlestubs between thumb and forefinger, just above a flame, and watched the meltings add themselves to the already considerable cone of wax and tallow which they had developed on the plate. The shining melt spilled roundly, rambling and congealing; wherever it ridged, they smoothed it delicately with their fingertips. From the apex of this rounded cone sprang three long fiery wicks.

Because they were to be up all night these two had been forgiven the fast and had supplied themselves against possible hunger. But neither had yet eaten or drunk, nor did either privately intend to unless, as seemed unlikely, he became too faint or too sleepy to attend properly to his share of the work. Their coffee frothed so noisily over its can of Sterno rather because this enhanced their feeling of privilege and maturity; Willard was drinking some while he talked although, Richard reflected, it was long after midnight, when the fast began. He had also practically finished off a box of Fig Newtons.

The coffee was so strong that it empurpled the wall of the cup, and its smell was almost as enviably masculine as that of white lightning. The three younger boys kept respectfully quiet and looked on, eagerly and sleepily. They watched now the lapped purple rings in the slanted cup, now the shining of the living wax and its satin look where it had slowed and had been smoothed, now the strong loose smoky flame and the hypnotized faces which leaned above it, and now the reckless primitive profile and the slash-lined blue-black cheek of the great athlete Willard Rivenburg, whom they had never seen in quite such quiet intimacy. Nobody knew for sure just how old Willard was, but he looked as many men can only at thirty or so, and then only if they have been through a war, or years of the hardest kind of work. Richard tried to imagine why he was here tonight. He was fairly sure it was not for any kind of religious reason: Willard had been confirmed, and made his Confession and his Communion, but it was obviously just as a matter of course; when he took his turn serving Mass or swinging the Censer or carrying the Crucifix he was never exactly irreverent yet he always looked as if secretly he might be chewing tobacco; it looked as odd and out of place, somehow, as watching a horse dressed up in cassock and cotta and doing these things. He never even crossed himself at a hard time in a game, the way some of the others did. No, he wouldn't be here because he felt pious. It might be because everybody and everything on the place was thinking about just these things that were happening, and moving around them; a kind of shadow and stillness came over everything during Holy Week and it might be that Willard felt this and was made uneasy by it. But mainly it must be just that he was much too grown-up to be able to stand all the silly rules, and tame hours, and good behavior, that were expected of living in a school; he must be even gladder than the little boys were to grab at any chance to break out of that routine, especially anything that would give him an excuse for staying up so long after hours. And yet, Richard reflected, Willard needed and took an awful lot of sleep, dropping off in dull classrooms or wherever he had to sit still, except for eating, as easily as a colored man or a dog. But maybe all that sleep was why he was able to be awake now, though as a matter of fact he wasn't really more than half awake, not nearly as wide awake as Richard felt. But then probably he had been up all night, and probably it wasn't for the first time in his life either.

In some way which it did not occur to him to think about or try to understand, Richard felt a warm rich comforting kind of pride in him and sense of glory as he watched him, as much, in a far quieter and even happier way, as when he watched his almost magical ability in sports; and he began to feel a sense of honor and privilege in having this surprising chance to be so near him and to watch him so closely, to really see him. For normally, when Willard was not playing or practising or sleeping or eating, he was kidding with somebody, in a loudly reckless, crazy way which was a pleasure to see because everything Willard did was a pleasure to see, but was impossible to see through; but now he wasn't kidding at all, only talking quietly and steadily like a grown man, among others whom he treated as grown men. He was finishing up about his grandfather who had come over from Switzerland to settle

way back on the Mountain and who had never bothered to learn much English, and he was saying the
few words and phrases of German he himself knew,
and Richard was deeply impressed in realizing that
Willard, who always seemed to him to know about
as little as anyone could, except as an athlete and cap-
tain of genius and a powerful and experienced man,
actually knew words in a foreign language. He himself was accustomed to feel a good deal of complacency because with Father Fish's help he had learned
several hundred words of French, but now he felt
ashamed of himself, and resolved to learn German,
which seemed to him a much more virile language.

He was watching with shy and particular interest
the hump between Willard's heavy shoulders, which
he had often wondered about but never yet had the
chance to examine so privately. It was almost as if
Willard were slightly hunchbacked, the low way he
always carried his head and sloped his shoulders and
the way this hump bulged out just below the base of
his neck; yet if he were deformed, he could not have
such ability and strength. It must be a very greatly
developed muscle, Richard realized, yet it was a
funny place to have a muscle; he felt there now on
his own body and there wasn't even the beginning
of a muscle there; just bone. Could it be bone? But

that would be a deformity; and on Willard, more than any other thing, it was what made him unique among others, and marked his all but superhuman powers. Whenever he had done anything physically creditable Richard carried his head low, let his mouth hang open, and tried to hump his back, scarcely knowing of it any more; and so, though it was not generally realized, did many other boys in this school.

"Hey you," Lee said, and startled, they looked: one minute past four. Richard felt a spasm of shame: could ye not watch with me one hour? Besides, they were keeping somebody over his time. "*Jesus!*" Hobe Gillum said, and they stood up quickly. Both of the boys in cassocks ducked in shocked acknowledgement of the Name and Willard's dark face brightened with his satanic parody of falsetto laughter. Lee Allen said with unusually kind gravity: "I sure would hate to have to report anyone for cussn right in Chapel, and on Good Friday too." Hobe's eyes turned Indian, with pride towards Willard, in defiance towards Lee. "Aw forget about it Lee," George Fitzgerald said, "he just wasn't thinking." "I don't want to report you or nobody else," Lee said. "You just watch your mouth, Hobie." "He didn't mean anything," Richard said; and even before everyone looked at him and said nothing, he was miserable. "Better put your shoes on you kids," George said, and with relief Richard sank his hot face over his shoelaces. They felt contempt for him, he was sure, and he felt contempt for himself. Willard thought better of Hobe for cussing than of him for standing up for him, and so did he. Lee jumped on Hobie because Willard's cackling about it bothered him and he couldn't jump on Willard. If it hadn't been Good Friday and Richard had spoken up like that he knew that somebody would have said coldly, "Well look who's talking." Keep your mouth shut, he kept whispering within himself intensely. Just keep your fool mouth shut. And as they left the room he tried to exorcise the feelings of injustice, self-pity and pain by crossing himself quickly and surreptitiously. Fine time to go worrying about your*self*, he sneered at himself.

The nave replied to their timid noises with the threatening resonance of a drumhead. Not even the sanctuary lamps were lighted, but the night at the windows made just discernible the effigies and the paintings and the crucifix, no longer purple veiled but choked in black, and the naked ravagement of the High Altar. The tabernacle gawped like a dead jaw. By this ruthless flaying and deracination only the skeleton of the Church remained; it seemed at once the more sacred in dishonor, and as brutally secular as a boxcar. To cross its axis without the habitual genuflection felt as uneasy as to swim across a sudden unimaginable depth, and as Richard turned and bowed before the central devastation he realized: nothing there. Nothing at all; and with the breath of the Outer Darkness upon his soul, remembered the words: And the Veil of the Temple was rent in twain.

But here in peace and victory before the adoration of all creatures past and breathing and uncreated, shrined and enthroned, starred round with unabating light and with the stars of all the fields of spring as well, exiled there yet abides throughout this night the soul and substance of the everliving God Who shall, within these few hours now, be restored to His High Altar and there devoured, leaving His whole Church desecrate and unconsoled until the hour of His glorious Resurrection from the Dead. Tied in its white veil, stifled, a huge masked Head, a thinly clouded Sun, the monstrance stood from the top of the tabernacle and broke at its center a dense tissue of flowers and light: candles it seemed by thousands, spear-high and merely tall, and short, and guttering, each an abiding upright fiery piercing and, crisp and

wearying, withering, dying, the frugal harvest of the
dawn of the year: from faint orchards the last apple
blossoms, still tenderly raveling their slow-borne
blizzard; branches of mild-starred dogwood and of the
hairy wild azalea, pink and white, from the mulled
gray woods, and little fistfuls of those breathless
violets which break the floor of winter, even the rare
mayapple, the twinleaf, whose bloom stays just a day;
and, of the first shivering domestic flowers, cold
jonquils, crowds of them, greenish with chill or
butter yellow or flaming gold, and clear narcissus,
reaching, bowing, staring, fainting in vases and jars
of metal and glass and clay and in drinking glasses
and mason jars and in small and large tin cans, all
these each in their kind and sufferance bore witness
before God while they might. Few of these early
flowers have strong fragrance, or any, yet the heat
and the brightness and the fragrance brought forth
by the burning wax and tallow and by the heat in the
closed room, all one wall of dizzying dazzle, were
such that it was at first almost as difficult to breathe
the freighted air as to breathe water, and this air was
enriched the more by the devotions of those who
knelt subsumed within the trembling light; and at
the instant of stepping into this hot and fragrant gold,
going upon one knee and gazing upon the blind

rondure of the monstrance and the thousand-pointed blossoming of fire and flower, his heart was lifted up and turned vague and shy as the words broke within him, upon each other, God: Death; so that the two were one. Death: Dead, the word prevailed; and before him, still beyond all other stillness, he saw as freshly as six years before his father's prostrate head and, through the efforts to hide it, the mortal blue dent in the impatient chin. He remembered within this instant how for the first time he had been convinced, and how eternally convincing it had been, when he saw how through that first full minute of looking his father had neither stirred nor spoken, and how the powerful right hand had lain half open against the exact center of his body; the cloth of his coat was not moved by any breathing and it was as if the hand were only a magically expert imitation of a hand, a hand of wax and, now looking again at the head, lips and a face of wax, a dent of wax, a head of wax immense upon this whole rich waxen air. Dead, the word came again, and shutting his eyes he prayed swiftly for his father the prayer of all his childhood, God bless daddy and keep him close to Thee and may light perpetual shine upon him, Amen; and casually, obliviously, as a trout into shadow, the image and memory vanished. It is Our Lord's death

today, he said to himself, but at this moment he could
see neither face, that of his father, or that of his Lord;
only the words returned, God: Death.

No praying-benches were available at first, and
they knelt where they entered, the waxed floor
brutal against their bones. In the Name of the Father
and of the Son and of the Holy Ghost, Richard
whispered rapidly to himself, moving his lips and
closing his eyes again. He crossed himself with care.
There was a sound of arising and departure and
through his eyelashes he saw Knox Peyton complete
his genuflection and step ungainly between him and
Jimmy, trying to subdue the reproach and annoyance
in his face. They stayed where they knelt, all on
their good manners before the one empty bench, and
Richard heard the whispered "go on" several times
before he realized that it was directed at him. Two
worshipers glanced unhappily behind them, shut
their eyes, and tucked their chins down, trying hard
to pray. "I be damned if I will," Richard thought,
and caught himself; he shut his eyes tightly and in
despairing shame tucked his own chin down. "Go
on," he heard. He decided that he ought to make a
penance of it. Trying to look and to feel neither
humble nor proud he crossed himself, got up, genu-

flected, tiptoed to the empty bench, genuflected, knelt, and crossed himself. Mr. Bradford closed his eyes, frowned, and deeply bowed his head. Home stretch, Richard said to himself, and quickly begged forgiveness for an irreverence which had not been premeditated but spontaneous. But wasn't it even worse to be so unaware of where you were that such a thought could occur spontaneously? Mr. Bradford completed his devotions and tiptoed towards the door, his eyes downcast. His effort to stay within himself was too successful; Richard heard him bump against one of the two boys, and his whispered accusing apology, and their feckless and ill-subdued reply. Deaconess Spenser, at the desk opposite his own, compressed her lips, crossed herself, got up, genuflected, and stepped behind him; he could hear the harsh whispered reprimand whistling through her false teeth. He looked carefully at his clasped hands, but he heard movement as the door was cleared and along the side of his eye Jimmy advanced and swiftly established himself at the newly empty bench and the Deaconess, her wattles a violent red and her mouth pulled in tight, returned to her own bench, genuflected, knelt, crossed herself, and sank her forehead into her hands. Behind him somebody else stood up and he heard the knee touch the floor and, knowing he ought not to, glanced back;

it was Hog Eye Kelsey, one of the littler boys from his own dormitory; already Hobe was standing to replace him. Not Hog Eye, he told himself; he can't help it: Jeff.

Pay attention, he told himself. Mind your own business.

He looked at the veiled monstrance; the brightest threads of the veil sparkled like mica, gold-white on silver-white, and in one place a rigid shaft of metal radiance almost pierced the fabric. One azalea bloom strayed against it as if it were straining to be near it. Tiny threads sprang out of the flare of the blossom, the way small straight lines are drawn in a funny-paper to show music coming out of a horn. An apple-blossom fell. Looking at the tired sleepless flames of the candles, Richard felt as if he could almost hear them burning.

Soul of Christ sanctify me, he prayed silently; Body of Christ save me; but he was just saying it mechanically, and too fast. Slowly now, thinking carefully of each word, he began again.

Soul of Christ sanctify me: make me holy: absolve me from all spot of sin:

Body of Christ save me: save me: Thy Body which has already begun to suffer and die:

He braced his mind.

Blood of Christ inebriate me:

Carefully as he tried, he could not avoid it. Inebriate meant just plain drunken, or meant a drunken person, especially habitual drunkard, and as it was used here, it meant to make drunk, to intoxicate. And inebriety meant drunkenness and the habit of drunkenness. He had been fond of the word for a long time before he knew, or realized that he did not know, its meaning — which must of course be simply what the Blood of Christ might most naturally be expected to do: but what would that be, that sounded as nice as inebriate? During the past winter it had occurred to him to look it up in a dictionary. Since then the correct and disconcerting meanings had been indelible, and that part of the prayer had become thin ice. He could only get past it without irreverent or skeptical thoughts by saying it so fast or so shallowly that it was impossible to bear its meaning in mind, and that was no way to pray. He had asked Father Fish about it and Father Fish had shown him that it was possible to be amused by the word without feeling irreverent. He had said that some of these ancient prayers were rather extravagant in their way of putting things, and that there was no need to take them with absolute literalness. Although he had no way of being sure, Richard had a feeling that Father Fish had been as amused at him, as at the word; once again he wondered why, and stopped himself from wondering why because this was no time to. Don't take it literally, he told himself firmly; but the literal words remained and were even more firm: make drunk. Intoxicate. Good ole whiskey, he suddenly heard in his mind, and he remembered how, drinking sodapop in Knoxville, boys slightly more worldly than he would twist the bottle deep into the mouth and cock it up vertically to drink, and taking it down, breathless, would pat their stomachs or rub them in circles and gasp, "Ahhh, good ole whiskey!" But this wasn't even on whiskey. On blood. Jesus' blood, too. His uncle had once sneered, "There is a pudding filled with blood," scornfully exploding the first syllable of "pudding," and Richard had been both shocked and amused, and he was shocked to find that he remembered it with amusement now. Forgive us our trespasses, he whispered, shutting his eyes tight. It was only a hymn, and so it was not as bad to make fun of as some things were. But the blood was "drawn from Emmanuel's veins," so that did make it pretty awful. And his uncle had said it with a kind of hatred which included much more than the hymn: all of religion, and everybody who was religious, even his own sister, Richard's mother, and his Aunt Patty, and him, Richard, and his own sister. Forgive us our trespasses as we forgive those who trespass against us, he prayed, and pushed the matter out of his mind. He does like us all the same, he reflected, same as grandpa does. They just don't like the Church.

Passion of Ch——

Water from the side of Christ wash me; and he felt that his thoughts badly needed washing:

Passion of Christ strengthen me:

Within Thy Wounds hide me, he thought swiftly and with great uneasiness, hugging the ground and the leaf coverage as if beneath the skimming of a bird of prey: but try as he could, the image plunged and took him. An older boy, the only one Richard knew who also liked to read, had with great sophistication and delight explained to him what was meant, in Shakespeare's *Venus and Adonis*, by the words *he saw more wounds than one*, and this had instantly become identical in his mind with a rawly intimate glimpse he had had, three or four years before, of Minnielee Henley when they were climbing a tree; and now with these words *within Thy Wounds hide me* the image fought in his mind with the image of those small but deadly wounds in the body of Jesus, in which surely nobody could hide, not even the one the spear made in His side. But not there either, he insisted to himself; not even if He wasn't a man. Yet there in his mind's eye, made all the worse by all the most insipid and effeminate, simpering faces of Jesus that he had ever seen in pictures, was this hideous image of a huge torn bleeding gulf at the supine crotch, into which an ant-swarm of the pious, millions of them, all pleading and rolling up their eyes, laden souls, by thousands meekly stealing, struggled to crowd themselves, and lose themselves, and drown, and dissolve.

It was the Devil, that was all. Just the Devil Himself, tempting him.

O good Jesu hear me, he prayed with deep self-loathing, almost aloud: and realized with gratitude that for once he had been able to say these words, which for months now had seemed to him fulsome and insincere, with complete desire and sincerity. You just have to mean it, he thought, for it to mean anything.

Suffer me not to be separated from Thee (a mortal sin is a sin that cuts us off from God):

From the Malicious Enemy defend me:

Of these closing lines he never felt doubt and now he repeated, with reverent emphasis and relish:

From the Malicious Enemy defend me:

In the hour of my death call me and bid me come to Thee:

That with Thy

No there was something really wrong about

He prayed, with fear and determination: That with Thy Saints I may praise Thee, forever and ever, Amen.

All the same it was wrong for people to ask to be saints, as flat as all that. Or even just to be *with* the saints, if that was what it meant. To just barely manage through God's infinite mercy to escape burning eternally in the everlasting fires of Hell ought to be just about as much as any good Catholic could pray for; and now Richard remembered still another prayer at which, when he was serving at Mass, he had for quite a while now been accustomed to keep silence or at most to make approximate sounds of the words, with his fingers crossed: where, in the General Confession, reviewing his iniquities, the penitent cries, "The remembrance of them is grievous unto us, the burden of them is intolerable." As a rule he was able to say "the remembrance of them is grievous unto us" with adequate sincerity; but it was seldom that he could feel, at the particular moment he felt required to feel, that "the burden of them is intolerable." It wasn't anywhere near intolerable, no matter how much it ought to be. At first he had been able to say it in the realization that it was intolerable to his soul, whether or not he in his mind and feelings was capable of feeling it just then, and that prayers are said by and for the soul, not the mind or the feelings; but in this he came to feel that he was mistaken: for it was, he noticed, only when he believed and felt deeply with his mind or his emotions that he was able to be aware that his soul, as such, existed. But that isn't true, he now thought with alarm. No matter what I think or feel, the soul is always there and always alive unless it has been killed by impenitence for mortal sin. The hardening of the heart towards God. I'm only trying to suit myself, he told himself; not my soul, and not God.

But how can you say things when you only ought to mean them and don't really mean them at all?

Have mercy upon us O God have mercy upon us, he found himself praying. These were the words of the Confession which followed "the burden of them is intolerable," and always, as now, he was able to mean them when he spoke them.

But not "that with Thy Saints I may praise Thee."

Now it occurred to Richard that perhaps this prayer had been written by a saint or by someone near sainthood, who was able to mean every extreme thing that was said; and he knew that anyone who could fully mean those things, and who could mean them every time they were said, was to be humbly respected. But in that case it was a prayer which was good only for saints and near saints to say, not for ordinary people, no matter how good they hoped to be. Nobody's got any business even hoping he can be a saint, he told himself.

God no!, he exclaimed to himself, for now suddenly it became vivid and shameful in his memory that he himself had for a while cherished, more secretly even than his lust, exactly this inordinate ambition. Good golly!, he whispered within his soul, feeling the back of his neck and then his cheeks go hot; and with a cold and marveling, compassionate contempt for the child he had so recently been, he lost himself in reflective remembrance, unaware that it was for the first time in his life.

It was hardly more than a year ago, when he was only eleven, that the image and meaning of Jesus and the power and meaning of the Sacraments and of the teachings of the Church, all embodied and set forth in formalities of language and of motion whose sober beauties were unique, and in music which at that time moved and satisfied him as no other music could, had first and, it had seemed, irreducibly, established upon all his heart and mind their quality, their comfort, their nobility, their sad and soaring weight; and, entering upon his desolation of loneliness, had made of suffering a springing garden, an Eden in which to walk, enjoying the cool of the evening. It had become a secret kind of good to be punished, especially if the punishment was exorbitant or unjust; better to be ignored by others, than accepted; better still to be humiliated, than ignored. He remembered how on mornings when he had waked up and found his bed dry, he had felt as much regret as relief. He had begun to take care to read in conspicuous places, where he would be most liable to interruption and contempt. He had pretended not to know lessons he had in fact prepared, in order that even such teachers as thought well of him, or thought "at least he's smart," or "he studies, anyway," might think ill of him. He had continued his solitary wanderings in the woods until it occurred to him that these excursions, for all their solitude and melancholy, were more pleasant than unpleasant; from then on he had put himself into the middle of crowds, especially on the drearier afternoons when even the hardiest boys stayed indoors and the restive, vindictive, bored, mob feelings were at their most sullen and light-triggered.

The leaden melodies of the Lenten hymns had appealed to him as never before; lines in certain hymns seemed, during that time, to have been written especially for him. *Jesus, I my Cross have taken,* he would sing, already anticipating the lonely solace of tears concealed in public: *all to leave and follow Thee; destitute, despis'd, forsaken,* were words especially dear to him; *Thou from hence my All shalt be.* As he sang that he felt: nobody else wants me; and did his best to believe it, even of his mother. He remembered now that this kind of singing had satisfied him most at Stations of the Cross, on cold rainy nights. *Perish ev'ry fond ambition,* he would sing magnanimously; (no I *won't* become a naturalist; I'll never explore the sources of the Amazon; I'll never even own a monkey, or be junior tennis champion); *all I've thought or hoped or known;* then tears and their subdual rewarded him: *Yet how rich is my condition* (never to live at home again, never to be loved or even liked), *God and Heaven are still my own;* and he saw crowned God and Heaven shining and felt, in a humble kind of way, that he literally owned them. Now remembering it he shook his head almost as if in disbelief, but he knew it had been so. Everything. He had done just about everything he could think of. He had gone seldom to Father Fish's cottage, for friendliness was certain there, and often cookies and cocoa too, and he had found that these luxuries meant most to him, in his desire to suffer for religious advantage, only when they were indulged so rarely that even while they were being enjoyed they enhanced the bleakness of the rest of living. He even schemed to intensify his always all but annihilating homesickness to the utmost possible, asking permission of the Master of the Day the more often, that it be the more curtly or impatiently or, at best, contemptuously refused; watching his mother's cottage, the one place he was almost never allowed to go, sometimes by the hour; sometimes in ambush under dripping trees, relishing the fact that only he knew of the miserableness of that watch; sometimes openly, hanging against the fence, relishing the fact that she knew, and others could see, and that even though she knew, she would try to ignore him and stay out of his sight, and that when at last she could ignore him no longer, she would hurt him by trying to be stern with him as she told him to go away, and would sharpen his unhappiness into agony by her idea of a sensible explanation why this senseless cruelty had to be law. "Because dear, mother thinks it's best for you not to be too near her, all the more because you miss her so much." "Because your father — isn't with

us." "Because mother thinks you need to be among
other boys Richard. In charge of men." And worst
of all: "I know how hard it is now but I know that
when you're older you'll understand why I did it,
and thank me for it." *Thank her!* his heart sneered
now, in bitter paroxysm. And for a moment so brief
that the realization did not stay with him, he felt hatred and contempt for his mother, for her belief in
submissiveness and for her telling him, on certain in-
furiating occasions, that it is only through submitting
bravely and cheerfully to unhappiness that we can
learn God's Will, and how most truly to be good.
God's Will, he thought now: I bet it isn't just for
people to be unhappy! Who wants to be *good! I* do,
he answered himself. But not like that. I sure was
crazy then, he thought, pleased that he was now able
to recognize the fact. Just a crazy fool. The whole
crazy thing had begun to fade away soon after
Easter, with the good weather, and had vanished so
completely during the free summer in Knoxville that
he had forgotten the whole of it until just now: but
all through that dreary winter and increasingly
throughout that drizzling season of penitence, he realized now with incredulous and amused self-scorn,
he had ever more miserly cherished and elaborated
his wretchedness in every one of its sorry ramifica-

tions, as indispensable to the secret, the solution, he had through God's Grace discovered; and had managed easily to forgive himself those parts of his Lenten Rule which he meekly enjoyed in public, by inventing still other, harder rules which were private. His mother had tried uneasily to suggest to him that there might be a kind of vanity mixed up in his extreme piety — "not that you *mean* it, of course, dear" — against which he must be on his guard; but remembering the role of dismayed parents and scornful villagers in the early lives of many of the saints, he had answered her gently and patiently, with forbearance, that was the word, as befitted communication between creatures of two worlds so unbridgeably different. He had been tempted on more than one occasion to say to her, "Woman, what have I to do with thee? Mine hour is not yet come"; but he had suspected that this might be thought impudent or absurd or even blasphemous. Nor had he ever said aloud, when others jeered or tormented, "Father, forgive them, for they know not what they do"; but had often fortified himself with the silent words, "And He held His peace."

It had only gradually been borne upon him that he himself might aspire to actual sainthood; he had quickly realized that if that was to be his goal it was necessary, starting young, he might already be too late, to perform in private for God's eyes alone and in public that others might see, and be edified, and remember, and revere him, a long and consistent series of remarkable spiritual feats. Let your light so shine before men that they may see your good works and glorify your Father, Which is in Heaven. But meditating what these might be, he had realized that there in truth he did run the danger of sinning through Pride, as those people do who look hungry when they fast; whereas his own ambitions were prompted (or so it seemed) by true religious feeling and by nothing else. These ambitions had crystallized during the late weeks of Lent, into a desire to do for Jesus as much as Jesus was doing for him and for all souls. He had experimented with extra fasting, but it was not possible to carry this far, since it was virtually impossible to be excused from meals without the sin of lying, and almost as difficult, he found, to sit at the table without eating, or eating little enough to give the fast any dignity or meaning. So he had chosen self-mortification instead. He had gone into the woods and eaten worms, but this had disgusted him, and he had been even worse disgusted when, on one occasion, he had come near tasting his own excrement. It had suddenly struck him as very doubtful indeed that Jesus would ever have done any such thing, and he had thrown the twig deep into the bushes and had carefully buried the filth. Efforts to scourge himself had been moderately painful but not sufficiently effective to outweigh the sense of bashfulness, even of ridiculousness, which he felt over the clumsiness of the attempt, in relation to the severity of the intention. So he had been reduced, mainly, to keeping very bitter vigil over his thoughts and his language and over his sensuous actions upon himself, and to finding out times and places in which it would be possible to kneel, for much longer than it was comfortable to kneel, without danger of getting caught at it. (He had been as frightened, once, by such an interruption, as if he had been surprised in a sexual act.) It was during one of these protracted and uncomfortable sojourns on his knees that his mind, uneasily strained between its own wanderings and efforts at disciplined meditation, had become absorbed in grateful and overwhelmed imagination of Christ Crucified, and had without warning brought to its surface the possibility of his own crucifixion. He had been wondering with all of a sincere heart how ever he might do enough for the Son of God Who had done so much for him when suddenly, supplanting Christ's image, he saw his own body

nailed to the Cross and, in the same image, himself
looked down from the Cross and felt his weight upon
the nails, and the splintered wood against the whole
length of his scourged back; and stoically, with infinite love and forgiveness, gazed downward into
the eyes of Richard, and of Roman soldiers, and of
jeering Jews, and of many people whom Richard
had known. It was a solemn and rewarding moment;
but almost within the next breath he recognized that
he had no such cause or right as Jesus to die upon
the Cross: and turning his head, saw Christ's head
higher beside his own and a third head, lower, cursing; and knew that he was, instead, the Penitent
Thief.

But it was of course out of the question that in
a deep country part of Middle Tennessee, in nineteen twenty-three, he could actually manage to have
himself nailed to a Cross; and although (if he should
have the courage) he could undoubtedly nail his own
feet, and even one hand (if someone else would
steady the nail), his right hand would still hang free,
and it would look pretty foolish beside a real Crucifixion. With any proper humility he would be con-
tent merely to be tied up, as the thieves usually were,
and to hang during the three hours of Good Friday
that Jesus hung on the Cross. Even that would mean

a good deal, if only in token; the widow's mite, only it seemed rather more than the widow had managed; and he realized that many others besides himself would be moved, and impressed, and very likely improved, by the good example. It would be impossible of course to get a Cross without removing the image of Jesus from it, that big life-size one out in the vestibule, and that would be irreverent even if it were allowed. Or someone might make one for him but he doubted it. He might make one for himself if he could sneak into Manual Training Shop and get enough private time, only everybody knew he wasn't any good with his hands and simple as a Cross must be to make, they would just laugh at any that he would be likely to make. One of the school's gridiron bedsteads would be convenient for tying to, and very likely even more uncomfortable to hang against than a Cross, but he was forced to doubt, as with the nail-holding and the Cross, that he could manage the whole tying-up by himself, and as he thought of asking someone else to help him, he felt extraordinarily shy. As he singled over each of the few whom in any degree he trusted, or on whose affection he could at all depend, he became sure that there was not one who would co-operate in this, or even really understand about it. It would be necessary instead to anger and deceive people he disliked into doing it: but that, he felt, was both unlikely and sinful. If he got them mad they would do what they wanted to him, not what he wanted them to do, and he could not imagine how to suggest to them that the one thing he didn't want was to be stripped of his garments (except for a loincloth) and tied to a bedstead for three hours. And even if he should manage to, he would be tricking them into a sin, and that would be a sin of itself. It was easier just to imagine it as something already done, and as soon as he forgot about the problems of getting it done it was better, too.

There he hung, the iron bars and edged slats of the bed acutely painful against flesh and bone alike; but he made no complaint. Rather, his eyes were fixed steadfastly upon the expiring eyes of his crucified Lord, and his own suffering was as naught. There was a steady murmuring of scorn, pity, regard and amazement beneath him, and now and again a familiar face and voice was lifted, pleading with him or commanding him to come down. Father McPhetridge, the Prior, his wide red face reared up and told him that this was the most outrageous thing that had ever been done by a boy in this School and that he was to stop it immediately and come down and take his punishment like a man. He replied, gently and calmly, his voice all the more effective because of its quietness after all that indignant roaring, that "punishment" (he smiled at the word in his suffering) would have to come at its own good time; he would descend (with their help) promptly at three o'clock and not before; and would give himself up to his punishers without making a struggle. Scourge me, he said; paddle me with the one with holes in it; put me on bounds all the rest of the year; expel me even; there is nothing you can do that won't be to the greater glory of God and so I forgive you. The Prior, abashed, withdrew; Richard saw his whispering among the other monks and the teachers and his face was redder than ever, and their whispering eyes were on him. The football coach Braden Bennett, who had so often sneered at his music lessons; his face was changed, now: though with a scornful wonder, men see her sore oppressed. He looked straight back into those bullying eyes, with such quiet fortitude and forgiveness that the scorn and the wonder deepened, the wonder even more than the scorn. His mother pled with him to come down; she was even crying; and he was awfully sorry for her; but he shook his head slowly and, smiling gently, told her: "No, Mother, I deeply repent for making you

cry, and feel so badly, but mine hour is not yet
come." She collapsed with sobbing and the women
of the place crowded around her; they took her arms
and helped her as she walked away, all bent over.
Some day you'll understand, he told her within himself, and you'll thank me for it; and he knew the hap-
piness that comes only of returning evil with good.
Willard Rivenburg's deep dark jaw hung open and
Richard could overhear his whisper, to Bennett,
"Jesus that kid's got guts." George Fitzgerald, scarcely able to contain his tears, held up a sponge soaked
in vinegar, which Richard forgivingly refused; and
Hobe Gillum and Jimmy Toole and Parmo Gallatin
and Keg Head Hodges and the others looked at him,
glum but respectful; even if it was no more than po-
liteness, he realized, he would never be last again,
when they chose up sides. Through the half-open
Chapel door he could still hear the voice of the Three
Hour Sermon, Father Ogle's voice, and he realized
that the service had no more than an hour, at the outside, to go; but the voice sounded half-hearted and
sailed hollowly around the almost empty Church;
nearly everyone in the community was gathered here
in the vestibule, and there were some even from
nearby towns, and suddenly a photographer climbed
onto the sandstone font and aimed at him and flashed

a bulb. STRANGE RITES AT MOUNTAIN SCHOOL, he read: and, as blood broke scalding upon his nape, sank his face into his hands and prayed, in despair, *O God forgive me! forgive me if you can stand to!...*

For, musing upon his past vanities with affectionate scorn or even as with a scornful wonder, the scorn, the living vanity, of one who has put away childish things, and dwelling upon them in remembrance, he had dwelt once more within them (within Thy Wounds hide me), ensnaring himself afresh. For these later imaginations were not wholly remembrance; some were newly his, and only now, even in the very hour of Christ's own passion, he had yet again seduced his soul. If others, if any other in the world, should know those absurd imaginations of his heart: by his dread and horror in the mere thought, he knew his contemptible silliness. But God of course knew, and Christ Himself, even now when the Son was suffering and the Father, grieving that He might not take the Cup from Him, was hovering in love and sorrow, yes, engulfed, enchanted in woe though they were, They knew very clearly though, it now occurred to him, his secret was safe with Them. In insupportable self-loathing he squeezed his eyes so tightly shut that they ached, and dug his

chin as tightly against his throat as it would lock and
in blind vertigo, scarcely knowing his action, struck
himself heavily upon his breastbone, groaning within
his soul, *the burden of them is intolerable*. With the
second blow he realized, in gratitude and in a new
flowering of vainglory, that he had been surprised
into contrition so true and so deep that beside it
every moment of contrition he had ever known before seemed trivial, even false, and for an instant he
questioned the validity of every Absolution he had
ever been granted. Yet almost before this question
could take form, and even while his fist was prepar-
ing its third assault against his inordinate heart, this
new doubt was supplanted by a recognition that his
action was conspicuous and that it must seem to
others as affected, as much put on for outward show,
as he himself, observing others, had come to feel that
various mannerisms in prayer must be. Bringing his
fist against his breast in circumspection he opened his
eyes, raised his head a little, and without turning his
head, glanced narrowly around him through his eyelashes.

Nobody seemed to have noticed anything out of
the ordinary although he could not, of course, be
sure of those who knelt behind him. He bowed his

head again, twisting it a little to the right, lowered
his right shoulder and drew it back a little, and ob-
served from nearly closed eyes. He still could not
see those who knelt directly behind him but so far
as he could see, nobody seemed to have noticed him;
then he caught Hobe Gillum's coppery eye, and
blushed. He readjusted his head and shoulder and
watched Claude Gray, who knelt a little ahead of
him and to the right. Claude's head was flung far
back and was so twisted in adoration that the point
of his left jaw, bright gold in the candlelight, was the
most conspicuous and almost the highest part of it.
What was more, it was clear that he was praying, not
to the Blessed Sacrament, but to the small, shrouded
statue of the Blessed Virgin above the lavabo table;
and noticing now for the first time that a little cup
of violets stood on the plaster ledge at her feet, Richard was sure who had searched them out among the
wet dead leaves to honor that place. He looked at
Claude again, particularly at the tilted curly back of
the head and at the abandoned angle of the brightened jaw, and thought, He may really mean it, he
may not even know it but I bet he does, I bet he
knows it makes a picture and I bet he got it from
some picture of some saint or other. But if he did
really mean it, and no longer knew he was doing it,

then it was not fair to blame him. He was probably
thinking about his mother. It seemed a long time ago
he had lost his mother to keep on making so much
fuss about it but maybe he took things harder than
most people. Richard suddenly felt deeply ashamed
of himself in case Claude really was grieving and
praying for his dead mother, and he began to feel
pity for her and for Claude as well, but then he
remembered Claude's voice, which sounded more
girlish than a girl's even though it had changed, re-
citing to him the Litany of the Blessed Virgin in im-
passioned sugary tones; O most clement O most holy
O most sweet Virgin Mary; something of that sort
and a lot more besides. He had felt uneasy about
the whole thing and at the instant that Claude
brought such juicy emphasis to the words *mosst
sweett*, with such meticulousness about both t's and
pronouncing *most* like *moused*, Richard had decided
that he definitely disliked the whole prayer; and
looking at Claude now, he disliked it even more
thoroughly, and he decided that even if Claude was
genuine now in his praying, he did not trust that
kind of praying. He remembered his mother's gos-
siping about Claude once, his desire that the School
should put lace borders on the cottas and his special
attentions to the Blessed Virgin, and saying impa-

tiently, "Well what I can't see is, why doesn't he just — go on over to Rome!"

But now remembering the scorn and impatience which had been in her voice, and still watching Claude, with the long hair of the back of his head like a shabby chrysanthemum, tilted above the weak neck, he felt that Claude was pitiful, and that it was careless and cruel to think of him contemptuously, and as shameful to be watching him in this way, so unaware that he was being watched, or that he might look in the least silly, so defenseless, as it would be to peer at him through a keyhole. How do *I* know, he thought; he's probably praying all right, and even if he isn't I've got no right to look at him like this and ——

With this, something he could not quite remember, which seemed to be prodding at the edges of his thought, came abruptly clear. He remembered that he had started looking at Claude, and speculating with mistrust about the quality of his praying, because he himself had done something, without affectation, which might easily be misunderstood to be affected. He could not quite understand it but he was in some ignoble way trying to put off onto Claude something that was wrong with himself, or even worse, was assuming that Claude was doing wrongly what he knew he himself had not done wrongly; and worse even than that, he had so wandered and so lost himself in speculating about the weakness of another that he had degraded and lost his own moment of contrition, and had forgotten the very sin for which he was contrite, in committing still another sin of much the same kind. But now, although he could see the first sin, and the moment of contrition, and the second sin, quite clearly, they formed something more like a picture than a feeling, and there were too many things in the picture for him to look at any one of them really closely. He felt shame and a sort of astonishment. He wondered whether he would ever learn, from committing one sin, how not to commit another of the same sort even in the very moment of repenting it; and he felt that it was strange, and terrible, that repentance so deep and real as he knew that his had been, could be so fleeting. He felt deeply sorry and was filled with self-dislike as he saw what he had done, but he knew that the feeling was of a much shallower kind than that in which, without foreseeing it, he had struck his breast so hard. He thought of Jesus suffering on the Cross, but that deep and truest contrition was not restored; he looked again at Claude's unpromising head, and felt a mysterious sadness, which he could not quite understand, for whatever was imperfect and incompetent: Claude; poor little Dillon Prince, with his square-bobbed tow hair and his pink lashless eyes, forever crying or just over crying or just about to cry; a hen, with a wry neck which could never be straightened, standing as if shyly to herself in one corner of the chicken run, with one wing hunched; his own imperfect and incontinent mind and spirit; and again of Jesus upon the Cross, suffering and dying that all such imperfections might be made whole, yes, even the poor darn hen; and tears came into his eyes, which he relished, but he knew they had nothing to do with the deep contrition he was trying to recapture. Ye who do truly and earnestly repent you of your sins, he whispered almost aloud, and are in love and charity with your neighbors, draw near with faith and take this Holy Sacrament to your comfort, and make your humble confession to Almighty God, devoutly kneeling.

His heart opened. Almighty and everlasting God, he prayed, Maker of all things, Judge of all men (and he saw as in a wheeling rondure the shining of all things, the shadows of all men), we acknowledge and bewail our manifold sins and wickednesses (and they manifolded themselves upon the air between

earth and heaven like falling leaves and falling snow)
which we from time to time (and over and over,
morning and noon and waking in the night) most
grievously have committed in thought (the wandering mind, the lascivious image which even now
flashed before him), word (the words of obscenity
and of cursing) and deed (the shame and the violence of the hands) against Thy Divine Majesty
(flung upward like so many arrows and so much filth
against the dying Son upon His Cross and the in-
vincible Father upon His Throne), provoking most
justly Thy wrath and indignation against us (he
bowed his head deeply, with eyes closed, and the
entire sky hardened into one spear driving down-
wards upon his bowed neck, yet Christ upon His
Cross merely looked into his eyes without either
wrath or indignation). We are heartily sorry for
these our misdoings. The remembrance of them is
grievous unto us (O yes it is surely grievous), the burden of them is (God, forgive me, forgive me, make
them intolerable, intolerable), the burden of them
is intolerable (it is, Lord, Lord God I want it to be),
is intolerable. Have mercy upon us most merciful
Father have mercy upon us (and he pressed his
clasped hands tightly against his forehead), for Thy
Son Our Lord Jesus Christ's sake forgive us all that

is past (is past), and grant that we may ever hereafter serve Thee and please Thee in newness of life,
to the honor and glory of Thy Name, Amen.

That we may ever hereafter. Ever hereafter.
Serve Thee and please Thee. Serve Thee and please
Thee in newness of life. Forgive us all that is past.
All. Past. Ever hereafter, in newness of life. Serve
Thee, and please Thee. To the honor and glory of
Thy Name.

He was as peaceful and light almost, as if he had
just received Absolution. Keeping his eyes thinly
closed, tilting his head quietly back, he could see the
tender light of the candles against his eyelids, and
he became aware once again of the strong fragrance
of all the flowers. Dying, he whispered to himself.
Soon now. For me and for all sinners. O sacred
Head. He heard on his rose-mild blindness the in-
finitesimal flickering of the clock like those tiniest of
thorns which cannot be taken out of the skin by
thousands, by crown of piercing thorn. Opening his
eyes just enough to see, looking through their rain-
bow flickering of little sharpness, sharp flames on the
dark, thorn flames in thousands, each a thorn, a little
sword, a tongue of fire, standing from pentecostal
waxen foreheads; go ye unto all the world, a briar-
patch of blessed fires, burning, just audibly crack-

ling; no; the clock. Now pale flowers, round, in thousands, stared flatly among the thousands of sharp flames, as white and lonely on the humming gloom as organstops, gazed at too fixedly during a stupefying sermon, round and bright as wafers, consecrated Hosts, in the tiny burning and prickling of Time. He did not quite conceive of Time except as a power of measure upon the darkness, yet opened his eyes now and saw that it was almost twenty-five, twenty-three and a half, past four. The clock stood on the lowest step of the Altar. Its leather case was inlaid with silver wire almost as fine as hair, which outlined intricate flowers and leaves. It was his mother's, and it had been borrowed for use in the Lady Chapel, as it always was for this Thursday watch, because it was the most nearly silent clock on the place. Now that he looked at it he heard it the more clearly, a sound more avid and delicate than that of a kitten at its saucer, and now that he heard nothing else he saw nothing else except the face of the clock, hard, handless, staring white out of a shadow of trembling gold, like the great Host in a monstrance; and when once again he saw the hands, and the numbers, they showed that only two minutes of his watch remained. Could ye not watch with me one hour? Now he remembered the images and emotions into which he

had awakened, so acutely, that they were almost his
again; but now in some way they had hardened, they
stayed at some distance from him, and he began to
realize that during this entire half-hour his mind had
been wandering: there had been scarcely one moment of prayer or of realization. Hell of a saint I'd
make, he said to himself; and added with cold and
level weary self-disgust to the tally of the sins he
must soon confess, I swore in Lady Chapel in the
presence of the Blessed Sacrament. God be merciful
unto me a sinner, he whispered in his mind, crossing
himself.

Now for the first time he realized that his knees
were very sore. The small of his back ached. When
he moved, bending his back, shifting his knees, everything whirled hazily for a moment, then, with a kind
of sliding or shunting like the falling into plumb of
a weighted curtain, came clear and stayed still. I
guess that was nearly fainting, he thought, with sat-
isfaction. He searched the deep grooves in his knees
along the edge of the board and re-established them
exactly as they had been, and bore down on them to
make them hurt the more, and he found that it hurt
still more to keep his back completely straight and
still, than to move it at all. The pain made him feel

strong and reverent, and smiling he whispered silently to Jesus, "It's nothing to what You're doing."
Our Father Who art in Heaven, he began; he knew
now that he would stay another watch through.

Now it was half past four, but nobody moved.
Nobody wants to be the first, he thought. No they're
all praying, he told himself. I'm the only one noticed what time it is. Behind him he heard a sound
of stealthy entering and of knees coming quietly to
the floor. Now somebody will give up their place,
he thought. It ought to be me.

Claude tilted his head to the other side and now
Richard noticed the translucent lavender beads in
his hands. He heard somebody stir and stand wearily up and he knew by the rustling starch that it was
the Deaconess. She was in when I came. Been an
hour. Maybe more. Quit keeping tabs, he told himself sharply. None of your business. There was the
sound of her going away and the sound of another
entering. Pray, he told himself. I ought to give my
place. It was nearly thirty-three minutes after. We
beseech Thee O Lord pour Thy Grace into our
hearts, that ——

The sacristy door opened and there was Lee Allen.
He looked more grave and tired than before and he
avoided Richard's eyes with an aloofness which

abashed him. That as we have known the Incarnation of Thy Son Jesus Christ through the message of an Angel: Lee came silently to the middle and genuflected; then from where he stood, shifting the extinguishing cone in exact rhythm, he put out seven shrunken candles to the left and seven to the right. He genuflected again, and leaned the tall snuffer into the corner, and returned, and genuflected; then strode to the Altar in a quiet and mastering way, reached delicately among the interlocked flowers, and uprooted with each hand a smoking seven-branched candlestick. He genuflected once again and tiptoed out, shutting the door to softly with one shoe. Smoke crinkled from each dark candle as he went. There seemed to be scarcely fewer candles than before, there were so many. There would be others to change, five on each side; the rest were still tall enough. Through the message of an Angel, so by His Cross and Passion: he heard behind him the prudent raising of a window, and for the first time realized how suffocatingly hot it was, and that he was sweating. The sacristy door opened and there was George Fitzgerald. His eyes were softer and brighter with tiredness than before and his face was white and bright red in patches. He met Richard's eyes quietly and impersonally. He came to the middle and genu-

flected, and Richard could see that he was looking at
all the flowers before he moved. Some still had
strength and some were dying, and now he took two
vases of those which were dying, unmeshing them
with great care from among the others, and genuflected, and tiptoed out, shutting the door to softly
with his shoe. Petals flaked away as he went. The
living air touched the back of Richard's neck; now
it even cooled his forehead; and now, rank on rank,
the flames of the candles acknowledged the invading
night; more petals fell. Upon the fragrance of fire
and wax and fresh and dying flowers there stole the
purity of water from a spring. Snaffling it desper-
ately in an inept hand, somebody sneezed. Claude
tilted his head back the first way and started his
beads all over again. Richard heard the sound of
bare feet withdrawing and knew that it must be
Hobe and Jimmy. I haven't even said my prayers,
he realized. I'm going to stay, he told himself. Give
up your place, he told himself. You got no business
hogging it. As much business as: you got no business
thinking that either: as Claude with his head on one
side and those beads. Give up your place. Come
back. Kneel on the floor. The same person sneezed,
more violently but better stifled. Claude, straighten-
ing his head, laid his beads down carefully, got up,

stepped to the middle, genuflected, turned, looking like St. Sebastian, and went to the rear of the Chapel. Richard heard his careful sliding-shut of the window; the flames stood straight; Claude returned, and again began his beads at the beginning. Soul of Christ sanctify me, Richard began aimlessly; the sacristy door opened and there was Lee Allen.

Richard shut his eyes. O God forgive me that I can't do it right, he prayed. O God help me do it better now. Make me to love Thee and to know Thy suffering this day. For Jesus' sake Amen. He crossed himself meticulously and got to his feet; he was dizzy and for a moment his knees hurt very badly. He stepped out of the desk, genuflected, and turned, and all of a sudden he knew he would have to go out at least for a minute or two, he was much too tired to stay. When he turned to genuflect again at the door, Lee was lighting the second of the tall new candles.

The darkness was cool and stale. From where he stood beside the door of the Lady Chapel, looking back across the nave, he saw the spaced badges of blacker darkness where the Stations of the Cross hung veiled. Tall at his right shoulder, a Madonna stood, a blind black monolith. He walked silently

towards the middle of the transept, and now he could
see the white stops and keys of the organ. He stood
at the center, facing the stripped Altar; sure that it
ought not to be done, but in an obstinate and loyal
reverence, he put down one knee and then both knees
before the desolate shrine: until His coming again.

He bent his head deep towards the floor and heard
his voice whisper slowly and fearfully within him
the words which, he suspected, only a priest may
utter without blasphemy: For in the night in which
He was betrayed:

His skin crawled.

This is the night in which He is betrayed.

He felt the floor, bitter against his knees, and
whispered aloud, "This is the night in which He is
betrayed"; and with the whispering it no longer was,
and he whispered within himself, He took bread, and
brake it, and gave it unto His disciples, saying, Take,
eat, this is my Body which is given for you; do this
in remembrance of me.

He saw, and was himself, grown and vested, genu-
flecting, raising the consecrated Host, again genu-
flecting, while a bowed kneeling boy, who was also
himself, shook the three bells.

Likewise after supper He took the cup, and when
He had given thanks he blessed it, and gave it unto

His disciples, saying, Drink ye all of this, for this is my Blood of the New Testament, which is shed for you and for many for the remission of sins. Do this as oft as ye shall drink it, in remembrance of me.

And with the words For this is my Blood of the New Testament, he knelt so deep in burden of blood that no priestly image entered him, and whispered again, Which is shed for you, and for many, for the remission of sins. And slowly one by one, while his hands lifted, the words stood up within his silence,

O Thou Lord God my Saviour: ("my Saviour," he whispered):

Look down on this Thy child.

Lord bless (he tried); O Lord lift up (he tried); O Lord forgive Thy child.

He could just see the empty Altar. There were no more words.

Do this as oft as ye shall drink it, in remembrance of me.

No more.

"Look down on this Thy child," he whispered aloud.

Now his knees hurt very badly.

"For Jesus' sake Amen," he whispered, crossing his breastbone with his thumb. He stood up.

If he went into the vestry they would say, What
you doing up? They would tell him to get on back
to bed. Not mean about it because of the night it
was but they would tell him all the same. Because
it was the rule. Or maybe they wouldn't but if they
did and he didn't go on back to bed it would be even
worse than if they hadn't seen him. "I told him
Father," he heard Lee Allen say in his serious hollow
voice. "That's right Father," George Fitzgerald said,
nodding soberly. And that was always worse when
somebody had told you; Prefects. "What did you
stay out for then?" "I dunno Father." "Course you
know. Why did you stay out? Why did all of you
stay out, Toole? You heard me tell you all to come
straight back to bed." Where were they? He was
suddenly scared. If they had gone back it would be
even worse for him if he didn't go back too.
"Where's Richard?" "I dunno Father." "Course
you know, you all went together. Where is he?"
"Honest Father *I* dunno. Last I seen him he was still
in Lady Chapel." That ought to make it all right.
Still in Lady Chapel. He was late but it was because
he was praying. Can't whip anybody for that. "You
know what the rule is." No. He'd say that to him,
not them, him, at Council Meeting; they'd come back
in time. "You know what I told you: come right on

back to bed." "But I was staying a second watch Father. Ask Lee. Ask George if I wasn't." "I don't care what you were doing I told you to come straight back to bed and you didn't do any such thing. Now what have you got to say for yourself?" Or no, maybe he would look embarrassed and just mutter something about You see to it you do what you're told, and not punish him. Or no he would maybe look mad when he heard that about the second watch and say, "And you've got the nerve to use *that* for an excuse?" And yet the year before he had stayed a second watch and there had not been any trouble. But that year nobody had told him to come right on back to bed. That was the year three of the boys had never even showed up for the watch they signed for but went over to Lost Cove and got some whiskey.

If they'd gone on back he was in trouble already.

Breathing light, and the breathing shaken by his heart, with the greatest possible stealth he approached the vestry door and, stiffening beside the frame like an Indian scout, spied slopewise between the door and the jamb. George was carefully arranging wild azaleas in a Karo bucket. Lee was not there. Hobe squatted against the wall; Richard could see only his cheek, brown-orange in the light of the fiery mount of wax, which had grown much larger. Willard hung out all over the folding-chair; the quietly snoring head lay back and the blue chin was the highest part of it. Jimmy sat on the floor between his thighs; he looked very sleepy. Lee Allen came quickly out of the back passage at the far end and he seemed to look straight at Richard and Richard flinched away and froze, but it was clear by Lee's voice that he had not actually seen him. "Ought to wake up Burgy and send these kids to bed," he said. "They aren't doing any harm," George said. "*I* don't keer," Lee said, "but I don't want to get in no trouble either, you know what they told us." George said nothing for a little while and then he said, "Me neither," and after a while he said, "I don't want you to get in trouble, count of me, Lee. You send them out if you want to. Don't let me hinder you." After thinking, Lee said, "Nobody hindern me." After a little he said, "Where's Sockertees?" which was one of Richard's nicknames, and Richard felt his breathing go thin. And Hobe said, exactly as Richard had fore-heard him, "Last I seen him he was still in Lady Chapel." "Well he ain't there now," Lee said. "Probly went on back to bed," George said. "No," he reflected, "We'd a heard him go out." "Crazy kid," Lee said. Richard tried to be sure whether this was said in affection or dislike, but so far as he could see it was neither, just an indifferent statement of fact. Dislike would almost have been better; and now he knew that he could not go in, right after Lee's saying that, and that although he felt very lonely, and suddenly wanted very much to be in there with them where no fuss was being made about not going to bed, he wanted still more not to be anywhere near them or anywhere near anybody. Crazy kid: crazy kid; yet he could not go away, for they might say more about him. He could hear George saying, "Oh, he's a good kid" or even just "Oh, he's all right," and it made everything much better, he could almost have gone in; but George didn't say anything of the kind, or anything at all, he just seemed to accept it as a fact everybody knew; and after a little Lee said, "I got to thin out them candles some if they're goana last through"; and George did not answer, and Lee said, "I thought there was a whole box more of them," and George said, "Not that I know of": and Lee did not answer, and George said, "If you thin out the candles some, maybe it'll give the flowers a chance, anyhow. I sure do hate to see dead flowers"; and suddenly, frightened because he was spying, Richard shrank as small against the wall as he could, for someone had come out of the Lady Chapel and now he could make out that it was Claude and realized thankfully, He sleeps in St. Joseph's, he'll go out the front. And sure enough Claude came to the middle as if to bow or genuflect and stood there a moment and then tossed his head upward to one side in a peculiar, saucy way, and turned his back on the Altar and walked back up the middle aisle and through the vestibule door; and after a moment Richard could hear the outside door; and then nothing; and after his breathing was quiet again, he crossed the transept without pausing to bow, and went back into the Lady Chapel.

The prayer-desks were all taken; he knelt at the rear on the bare floor and crossed himself, and closed his eyes, and bowed his head. Lord make my mind not to wander, he prayed, successfully driving from his mind Claude's impudent head. This is the last chance, he told himself. By leaning a little he could just see the clock. Already it was nearly quarter of. He felt fury against himself and subdued it, for it was evil. God be merciful unto me a sinner, he prayed, shutting his eyes again.

He waited carefully with his eyes closed but nothing came to him except his emptiness of soul and the pain of his knees and of his back. Hail Mary, he whispered to himself, and went through the prayer twice. He repeated five more Hail Marys rather rapidly and then three very slowly, trying to allow each word its full weight, and still there was nothing, not even through the words Pray for us sinners now and in the hour of our death. What's wrong with me, he wondered. He kept his eyes shut. Perhaps exactly because he had given his knees a rest, they now hurt worse than ever. Or it was because they were now on the flat floor, instead of braced against the edge of a board. The grooves where they had been against the board hurt badly, the bones just below the kneecaps hurt even worse. And within another minute or so, the small of his back ached worse than it had before. He bent over a little, and though that hurt his back in a new way, it also gave it a sort of rest. He let himself slacken down so that his buttocks sat on his heels, and that at least changed the pressure on the bones of his knees. He leaned forward so that his chest almost rested against his knees, and that helped his back. It'll just look like at Adoration, he reflected; and was ashamed of his hypocrisy. All the same, he thought, if it'll help me pray. Hail Mary, he prayed again. But still there was nothing. His heart was empty and his mind was idle, and he could not forget his discomfort.

He opened his eyes and looked around for a kneeling-pad and he saw one, skated against the baseboard, ahead of him and across the Chapel. He would have to get up and go in front of Julian to get it, and Julian was not using one. He hasn't been kneeling as long as I have, he reflected. What of it. He'll think I came in late. Just now. What of it. But the more he thought about it the more clearly he decided he would not go over and get the pad. If I can't say my prayers right, he told himself, why anyhow I can do this. He felt proudly and calmly vindictive against himself. Closely attentive to everything he was doing, he raised himself straight onto his knees and he straightened his spine so that his knees and the small of his back should hurt as much as possible, and he put the heels of his hands together, the fingers extended, edge to edge, tips touching, and the right thumb crossed over the left, as he had been taught when he was learning to be an acolyte. Ordinarily this strange and careful position of the hands embarassed him, for it seemed sissy. Only a few of the servers kept to it; most of them, like Richard, simply folded their hands, and so did most of the priests; but now it seemed no more sissy than being on your knees in the first place. It was just the right way to hold your hands to pray, that was all. For all the aching in his knees and his back he was now even more clearly aware of his hands in this unaccustomed position, the palps of the fingers touching so lightly and competently, the locked thumbs, the cleanly hollow of shaded light within the palms; his hands felt full of goodness and quiet and they made him think of pictures of Cathedrals.

He tried to breathe so quietly that he could not feel his chest go in and out or even any air moving in his nostrils, and he gazed studiously at the monstrance, visualizing through the veil the spangling sunlike gold and the white center, and upon that center Christ Crucified, Whom he saw first in metal and then in wood and then in flesh; but he began to wonder whether these efforts at visualization were not mere tricks and temptations of emptiness, for still he was empty of prayer and of feeling. Now that he forbade himself images and dwelt within the discipline of his body his knees and his back began to hurt worse than ever and he began to think with quiet and increasing amazement of young men, boys really, hardly older than he was, not much older than George anyway, who knelt like this on Chapel stone the whole night through in prayer and vigil, their weapons and armor blessed and waiting, soberly shining in the lambent gloom, before the Mass and the Communion and before the greatest

moment of their lives when their King touched the
flat of the sword to the shoulder and the young man
stood up and was assisted in putting upon himself the
whole armor of God and rode forth into the glit-
tering meadows of daybreak for the first time a
knight, a knight errant, seeking whatever wrong God
might send him to set right, whatever tests of valor
and chastity the huge world might hold in ambush
for him. O but I can do better than this, he exclaimed to himself in self-contempt; and he thought
with envy and reverence of the early time which had
belonged to those shining young men, and he pressed
down with all his strength and weight, first on one
knee and then on the other, so that it was hard not to
cry out, and he held his back still more rigidly upright, and he was pleased to find that now, by the
way he held his hands out, even his arms ached, deep
into the shoulders. But it's so little to do!, he thought,
imagining the first, living Crucifix; and he did his best
to imagine one hand, against splintery wood, and the
point of a spike against the center of the open hand,
and a great hammer, and the spike being driven
through, breaking a bone, tight into the wood so
that the head was all buried in the flesh and the splintered bone, and then to be able to say, *Father forgive
them for they know not what they do*. And that's

just one hand, he reminded himself. How about both hands. And both feet. Specially both feet crossed on each other and one spike through both insteps. How about when they raise up the Cross with you on it and drop it deep into the hole they dug for it! And imagining that moment he felt a tearing spasm of anguish in the center of each palm and with an instant dazzling of amazed delight, remembering pictures of great saints, shouted within himself, *I've got the Wounds!* and even as he caught himself opening his palms and his eyes to peer and see if this were so he realized that once again this night, and even more blasphemously and absurdly than before, he had sinned in the proud imagination of his heart. *O my God*, his heart moaned, *O my God! My God how can You forgive me!* I'll have to confess it, he realized. I can't. Not this. How can I confess *this!*

The thing he had most dreaded to confess before, an impure act which in its elaborateness had seemed merely the more exciting in the doing and which was so nearly unbearable to specify to another, and a priest at that, that he had gravely considered the risk to his soul of merely generalizing it: beside this new enormity — and twice over in one night, and both times in the Presence — beside this, that ugly and humiliating lustfulness seemed almost easy to tell of. But I'll tell it all the same, he told himself grimly. Because if I don't I'm in mortal sin. No I'll tell it because I did it and I hate to so much, and I don't care who it is I have to tell it to either, I won't dodge whoever it turns out to be and wait for another, not even if it's Father McPhetridge. I'll tell the whole thing just the way it happened — way I thought it happened, that is. I'll tell it all right. Because I've got to.

He looked proudly at the monstrance and felt strength and well-being stand up straight inside him, and self-esteem as well; for it began to occur to him that not many people would even know this for the terrible sin it was, or would feel a contrition so deep, or would have the courage truly and fully, in all of its awful shamefulness, to confess it: and again the strength and the self-esteem fell from him and he was aghast in the knowledge that still again in this pride and complacency he had sinned and must still again confess; and again that in recognizing this newest sin as swiftly as it arose, and in repenting it and determining to confess it as well, he had in a sense balanced the offense and restored his well-being and his self-esteem; and again in that there was evil, and again in the repenting of it there was good and evil as well, until it began to seem as if he were tempted into eternal wrong by rightness itself or even the mere desire for rightness and as if he were trapped between them, good and evil, as if they were mirrors laid face to face as he had often wished he could see mirrors, truly reflecting and extending each other forever upon the darkness their meeting, their facing, created, and he in the dark middle between them, and there was no true good and no true safety in any effort he might ever make to realize or repent a wrong but only a new temptation which his very soul itself seemed powerless to resist; for was not this sense of peace, of strength, of well-being, itself a sin? yet how else could a forgiven or forgivable soul possibly feel, or a soul in true contrition or self-punishment? I'm a fool to even try, he groaned to himself, and he felt contempt for every moment of well-being he could recall, which had come of the goodness of a thought or word or deed. *Everything* goes wrong, he realized. Everything anyone can ever do for himself goes wrong. Only His Mercy. That's what He died for. That's what He's dying for today. Only His Mercy can be any help. Nothing anyone can do but pray. O God, he prayed, be *merciful* unto *me*, a *sinner*. Let me not feel good when I am good. *If* I am good. Let me just try to be good, don't let me *feel* good. Don't let me even *know* if I'm good. Just let me try. And in this humility, aware that it was of a true and pure kind which was new to him, he felt a flash of relief, well-being, pride: and tightening his shut eyes, cried out in despair within himself, *There it is again! O God make it go away. Make it not mean anything. O God what I can't help, please forgive it.* He wanted to put himself down on his face on the floor. "*All my trust I put in Thee,*" he whispered aloud and, aware that he had whispered aloud, opened his eyes in the fear that he had been noticed. Nobody seemed to have noticed. Now Jimmy and Hobe were kneeling a little ahead of him. He found that he was drenched with sweat and as short of breath as if he had been running. He felt weak and quiet. *The burden of them is intolerable.* He could feel the words sincerely and quietly now yet at the same time they meant nothing to him. All my trust I put in Thee, he repeated silently. O let me not fail Thee.

Tonight.

This very night.

For in the night in which He was betrayed.

Now fragments of his first moment awake returned but now they were dry and tired like dead leaves, as dry and tired as he was. He tried to realize what it all meant. But all that he could realize was dry and tired like the tired dry fire of the candles.

He came into the world to be with us and save us, and this is what happened. This is what it all came to.

The light shineth in darkness and the darkness comprehended it not.

He came unto His own and His own received Him not.

So there He was just sitting there waiting. Just waiting to die.

Words stirred and stood up inside him which lifted his heart: But as many as received Him, to them gave He power to become the sons of God.

And the Word was made Flesh and dwelt among us:

He closed his eyes and bowed his head.

Flesh.

All for us.

All his suffering for all of us.

He remembered the terrible thing his uncle had said: "Well who *asked* him to die for me? *I* didn't. He needn't try and collect on the debt," he had said, "because there's no debt, far's I'm concerned." Nearly always when he thought of this Richard was shocked almost into awe of such blasphemy; and some few times when some priest or his mother was insisting what we all owe Jesus he had been tempted to wonder, wasn't it maybe really so, for it was a fact; Jesus had done it without anybody asking Him to: but now it seemed neither blasphemous nor persuasive but only empty and idle and cruel and as he thought of it he could see the man of whom it had been said, sitting very quietly on a stool or maybe a bench among the iron-breasted helmeted soldiers while they hit him and spat in his face and mocked him. Nobody could come near him or help him or even speak a word of love or thanks or comfort to him now. He could see him only as if he spied down on what was happening through a cellar window and it would be torture and death to dare to even try to get in, and no use could come of it, even if he did. The way, maybe, Peter had stayed. All of Peter's betraying and cowardliness was over and done with now. Nothing could ever wipe out for him what he had done. He wasn't even crying any more because he couldn't even cry any more. He was just hiding around on the outskirts, spying through the window. He was afraid to show himself and he couldn't stand to go away. He must wish he was dead.

Judas, by now, had he hanged himself? Richard couldn't remember for sure when. But if he hadn't yet, that was all there was left for him to do. That was all he was thinking about all the rest of this night, all that was left of his life. I want to die. O I want to be dead. I can't be dead soon enough to suit me. Judas didn't feel contrition, Father Weiler said, he felt remorse. Probably he couldn't cry like Peter. Just terrible cold remorse, as cold and bitter as the sound of the word. Remorse is very different from contrition; a deadly sin. A mortal sin is a sin that cuts us off from God. With remorse you don't feel sorry like contrition, you feel, well you just feel remorse, that's all.

These were just the dead hours. The hours between. They must be the worst hours of all for Jesus and for everyone who loved Him. No more doubt now. No more praying to God the Father, if this Cup can be taken from me: that's over long ago. It can't. That's all. No more judgment, standing trial, answering fool questions. He's already been sentenced to die. He belongs to the Law. Now just the time between. So tired. No sleep all this night. Waiting, getting Himself ready inside, while they mock and sneer and holler at him, and spit in his face, and crown him with thorns, and put the reed in his hand for a scepter, just waiting through the rest of the long night, just getting ready to die, while the night slowly turns into morning, and it's the last morning of all. To suffer so he will cry out, *My God, my God, why hast Thou forsaken me?* And then die. *It is finished.* And then die. And meekly bowing down His head, He gave up the ghost. And then (Richard could remember in advance) the stunned and strange peacefulness, throughout that afternoon and night and through all the next day, and the quiet, almost secret lighting of the tremendous candle in the beginning of the dusk of Holy Saturday, everything still going as if on tiptoe, and then in the first light of morning, the stillest and most wonderful moment of the year, the quietly spoken and simple Mass: "He is risen." And then the rich midmorning and the blinding blaze of Easter. *'Tis the Spring of Souls today, Christ hath burst His prison, and from three days' sleep in Death, like a Sun hath risen.*

But not yet. That is still not known though at the same time it *is* known. We are all in most solemn sorrow and grief and mourning. We know a secret far inside ourselves but we don't dare tell it, even to ourselves. We don't dare to quite believe it will ever really happen again until it really happens again. Until His coming again. For in the night in which He was betrayed. It has happened over nineteen hundred times now and yet it has never happened before. Not yet. And we don't know if it ever can. Never dreamed it could. Can.

Not yet. Now is just the dead time between and he is waiting. This is his last night and his last day-break begins soon now. Before this day is over he will be dead.

My Jesus, he whispered, clasping his hands strongly; his throat contracted.

O Saviour of the World Who by Thy Cross and Precious Blood hast redee ——

O you are dying my dear Lord for me, his soul whispered, wondering, weeping. For *me*, and I can't do anything for you. I can't even comfort you, or speak to you, or thank you. O my Lord Jesus I can thank you. I can think about you. I can try to know what it is you are going through for me. For me and for all sinners. I can know that every sin I do big or no matter how little is a thorn or a nail or the blow of the hammer or even just a fly that teases and hurts you in your blood, crawling and tickling and sipping and eating at you in the hot day on the Cross with you unable to brush him away or even to move, and every good thing, or true thankfulness or thought of love must make it anyway a little less terrible to suffer. My Lord I love Thee. My Lord

I grieve for Thee. My dear Lord I adore Thee. My poor Lord I wish I could suffer for Thee. My Lord I thank Thee. Lord have mercy upon me. Christ have mercy upon me. Lord have mercy upon me.

He opened his eyes in quiet wonder. It was indeed to him the very day. Not just a day in remembrance, but the day. There stood His consecrated Body, veiled among fire and flowers, but also living, in the flesh, on this very morning, at this very moment, He was waiting; and He was now within His last hours.

He won't see the sun go down today.

He looked at all the lights, spearing, aspiring, among the dying flowers. Knobbled and fluted with their own spillings, the candles stood like sheaves; some, bent by the heat, bowed over like winter saplings. Almost all the flowers hung their exhausted faces. They were so shrunken and disheveled now that he could see clearly among them the many shapes and sizes of the vessels which held them, the professional vases and ewers and jars, and the tumblers and tin cans from the poor cabins out the Mountain. He could just hear the clock. Tonight, he whispered, watching that devastation. This night. This minute. He leaned, and looked at the clock. It was

one minute after five. Something troubled him
which he had done or had left undone, some failure
of the soul or default of the heart which he could
not now quite remember or was it perhaps foresee;
he was empty and idle, in some way he had failed.
Yet he was also filled to overflowing with a reverent
and marveling peace and thankfulness. My cup run-
neth over, something whispered within him, yet
what he saw in his mind's eye was a dry chalice, an
empty Grail. No more I could do, he reflected, if I
stayed all night. No more. No use: and he continued merely to look without thought at the em-
blazoned ruin. "Goodbye," something whispered
from incalculably deep within him. *O goodbye,
goodbye,* his heart replied. A strange and happy sorrow filled him. *It is finished,* his soul whispered. He
looked at the humbled backs ahead of him and
prayed: The peace of God which passeth all under-
standing keep our hearts and minds in the knowledge
and love of God, and of His Son Jesus Christ. And
the blessing of God Almighty, the Father, the Son
and the Holy Ghost, be amongst us and remain with
us always.

He opened his eyes; and it was all as it was before.
Of course it was. He was light and uneasy and at

peace within. There was nothing to do or think or say.

He signed himself carefully with the Cross, got up, genuflected, and left the Chapel; just inside the north door, he took off his shoes. Hobe and Jimmy came up behind him and they took off their shoes too.

THE
MORNING WATCH

⚜ III ⚜

THE
MORNING WATCH

III

THEY WALKED DOWN the sandstone steps
into an air so different from the striving candles
and the expiring flowers that they were stopped flat-
footed on the gravel. Morning had not yet begun but
the night was nearly over. The gravel took all the
light there was in the perishing darkness and shed it upward, and in the darkness among the trees below the
outbuildings a blossoming dogwood flawed like winter

breath. In the untouchable silence such a wave of energy swept upward through their bare feet and their three bodies into the sky that they were shaken as if a ghost had touched them. Sharply and almost silently, Hobe laughed.

They looked at the last tired stars and at the dark windows of their dormitory and they wondered what their punishment would be.

"S - - t fahr," Hobe said. "Can't even pray, what the f - - - *kin* ye do!"

Maybe, Richard reflected, they wouldn't say anything. Couldn't be a better excuse than praying. In brainless exaltation he flexed the soles of his feet against the ground. What of it if they do.

Rustily, so far down back of them across the fields they could scarcely hear him, a rooster crowed.

"Let's get the rackets," Richard said.

They took it as naturally as if one of them had said it.

"They'd catch us sure," Jimmy said.

"Hell we keer," Hobe said. "Tan our asses anyhow, now."

Creakily, a little nearer, but very faint, a second rooster answered.

Might not, Richard thought; not *anyhow*. What if they do.

"Let's go to the Sand Cut," Hobe said.

"Freeze yer balls off," Jimmy said.

"Sun-up, time we git thur," Hobe said.

Proud, fierce behind the cook's house, the cry of a third rooster shining sprang, speared, vibrated as gaily and teasingly in the centers of their flesh as a jews-harp.

"Come on," Richard said, and started walking rapidly across the pale gravel.

He was surprised that he had spoken and the more surprised to hear them following. How they do it, he thought, stepping along not quite steadily in silent uneasy elation; all there is to it. He led them down past the cook's house.

Pride, he realized; a mortal sin. How do I confess that?

Through the veering wire net he saw, black in the faintness, how the big rooster darted his vigilant head and shuffled his plumage: in the silence before daylight a priest, vesting himself for Mass. Something heavy struck and the whole body splayed, and chuckled with terror; the coward's wives gabbled along their roost.

Richard felt as if he had been hit in the stomach.

I'm scared of both of them, he reflected, specially Hobe, and they know it whenever they want to.

And bigger than either of them, he forced himself to recognize.

Younger. Big for his age that's why I'm clumsy and soft.

Bigger all the same.

Maybe that makes up for the Pride, he thought, as they walked past the bruising foulness of the back-house.

Privately, safe ahead of them, he struck his breast.

Nothing makes up for anything. Confess you thought it did.

He tried to imagine how to confess it. I have sinned the sin of Pride and some other sin I don't know the name of. I was proud because when I said let's go to the Sand Cut (and it wasn't even me that thought of it first) they came along just as if one of them had said it and all of a sudden I knew that all you have to do is say something and go ahead yourself without waiting and they'll do it. Then something happened that made me know I was scared of them and I admitted to myself I'm : yellow : and then I thought maybe because I made myself admit that, why then I wouldn't have to confess I was proud before. I thought it made up for it.

He tried to imagine the priests to whom he would confess this. Father McPhetridge, Father Whitman,

Father Weiler, Father Ogle, Father Fish. Unless maybe if he got Father Fish but even if you tried to dodge and choose which was probably a sin why you couldn't ever tell for sure who you'd get. The others would just think he was crazy or something. Crazy kid. Or trying to get credit. And maybe he would be.

What you say in Confession they never tell because if they do they go straight to Hell. But whoever you confess to, he knows all the same. And if he knows you honestly are trying hard to be good he gives you credit afterwards too, that you sin if you try to get, he can't help himself. And if he thinks you're just trying to get credit why everytime he looks at you from then on you know what he thinks of you.

If he really thought you were, though, probably he wouldn't give you Absolution.

If you know it's a sin why you've got to confess it, no matter what he thinks.

The ferment of the hogpen, deepest of blacks and heaviest of oils, so stuffed and enriched their nostrils that as one they slowed against the fence and looked in. Small as the light was, on all its edges the chopped muck shone like coal. Jimmy slid his hand inside his overalls against his naked body; becoming aware of what he had done, he thoughtfully withdrew it. Straining to see into the darkness of the shed they could just discern the close-lying egglike forms of the hogs.

"Oink: oink," Hobe grunted, in a voice so deep that Richard was surprised.

Crooomphth, a sleeping hog replied.

They crossed the stile and struck into the woods, using their unhardened feet somewhat delicately along the familiar path. It was as thrilling cold and as vague and silent here as leaving a hot morning and stepping into a springhouse, and the smell of dead leaves and decaying wood and of the arising year was as keen as the coldness. A dogwood dilated ahead of them, each separate blossom enlarging like an eye, and swung behind, and deeply retired among the black trees ahead they could see the shining of others in the first light, triumphal and sad, lonesome as nebulae; likewise blind clumps of unawakened laurel; and now as the light became adequate they saw that the floor of the woods was still the leathery color of last year's leaves, meagerly stitched with green. In the deeper distances the woods were neutral as a photograph, as they had been all winter, but nearer by, the trunks of the trees were no longer black. Some were blackish, some were brownish,

some were gray and gray green and silver brown
and silver green and now the forms and varieties of
bark, rugged, mosaic, deeply ribbed and satin sleek,
knobbled like lepers and fluted like columns of a
temple, became entirely distinct. Some of the twigs
looked still as dark and fragile as the middle of winter, many were knobbled and pimpled and swollen
as if they were about to break open and bleed, and
many were the color of bronze and some were the
color of blood; on some there were little buds like
the nubbins of young deer and on others new leaves
as neatly fledged as the feathering ought to be for
the arrows Richard had never been able to make perfectly. They could see a long way into the woods as
the morning cleared and everywhere underfoot this
leather laid its flat musing waves and everywhere
among the retreating trees strayed sober clouds of
evergreen and mild clouds of blossom and the dream-
ing laurels, and everywhere, as deep into the stunned
woods as they could see, layer above unwavering
layer, the young leaves led like open shale; while,
against their walking, apostolically, the trees turned.
The path among these winding, dancing trees, new
to them since late fall, was supple underfoot, the
droning trees against which they laid or slapped their
hands felt as alive as the flanks of horses, the air was

all one listening joy. While they approached the
clearing each held in mind a festival imagination of
the plum tree, but it hung black, all crazed elbows,
in the widened light. From somewhere, however,
the fallen silvers of the ruined house it seemed, they
were pursued by the chiding, familiar song of an
ambushed bird whose kind they did not know; and
at the far side of the clearing Richard stopped short
and the others passed him: for here, abject against
sharp bark, he found a locust shell, transparent silver
breathed with gold, the whole back split, the hard
claws, its only remaining strength, so clenched into
the bark that it was only with great care and gentleness that he was able to detach the shell without de-
stroying it.

It was as if air had been tightened into substance;
only by touch and sight, not at all by weight, could
he know he held it. He held it in his cupped hand
and looked at the hunched, cloven back, turned it
over with one fingertip and examined the brutally
elaborate structure of the legs and the little talons.
He tested: they could pierce a finger. He turned it
again and held it near his eyes: the eyes looked into
his. Yes even the eyes were there, blind silver globes
which had so perfectly contained the living eyes:
even the small rudimentary face in its convulsed and

fierce expression, the face of a human embryo, he could remember the engraving in a book of his grandfather's, a paroxysm of armor, frowning, scowling, glaring, very serious, angry, remote, dead, a devil, older, stranger than devils, as early, ancient of days, primordial, as trilobites. Dinosaurs heaved and strove; a pterodactyl, cold-winged, skated on miasmic air, ferns sprang, to make coal in these very coves, more huge than the grandest chestnuts. Silurian, Mesozoic, Protozoic, Jurassic, all the planet one featureless and smoky marsh, Crowns, Thrones, Dominions, Principalities, Archaeozoic, through all ranks and kingdoms, to the central height, armed in the radiant cruelty of immortal patience, Ages and Angels marched clanging in his soul.

When did he come out? Just now? Just this spring? Or has he stayed all winter. And that would mean all fall and summer before.

I'd have seen him; last fall; last spring.

If he was there all the time and I didn't before, how come I saw him now?

All winter. All year. Or just since the first warm weather. Or just now before I found him.

That whole split back. Bet it doesn't hurt any worse than that to be crucified.

He crossed himself.

He sure did hold on hard.

He tried to imagine gripping hard enough that he broke his back wide open and pulled himself out of each leg and arm and finger and toe so cleanly and completely that the exact shape would be left intact.

With veneration, talon by talon, he re-established the shell in its grip against the rigid bark.

By the time he caught up with Hobe and Jimmy they were almost to the railroad track.

At the far end of the break in the woods along the far side of the track they saw the weathered oak tower and soon, walking more briskly along the ties, the relics of machinery and the dead cones of putty-colored sand and the wrinkled sandstone and, at length, the sullen water itself, untouched in all these cold months. There were black slits along the sides of the tower where planks had fallen during the winter. The water was motionless and almost black. The whole place, familiar as it was, was deadly still, and seemed not at all to welcome them. As they left the track to round the near end of the Sand Cut there was a scuttling among the reddened brambles but although they went as fast as they could on their soft feet and threw rocks where the brambles twitched with noise they got no glimpse of whatever it was, and soon the scuttling stopped.

Now that they had stopped walking and stood in the brightened silence of the open light the day began to look practical; they realized how chilly the air still was, even here out of the woods, and how bitter the water looked, and they no longer felt like going in. But none of them was willing to admit this frankly even to himself, and it was only after they stripped that they became openly hesitant. They took care not to shiver more visibly than they could help or to appear to dawdle, either, but they did all dawdle, and they found that they were looking at each other, in this unhabitual place and hesitant quietness, with more interest than in the dormitory. Although Jimmy was the smallest of the three in every other way, his was much the biggest and during the winter he had grown much more hair than Richard had realized up to now. Hobe still didn't have much but then he was said to be part Indian so of course he wouldn't, yet, and probably never would have a lot. What he did have was dark, though, and showed up well against his dark skin, whereas Richard's was so light and there was so little of it that he realized it could probably not be seen at all, farther away than his own eyes. He suspected, however, that his was really the biggest, because it looked as if Jimmy had at least half a hard-up.

Jimmy looked comfortable in his supremacy whether
it was real or not (he certainly had more hair, anyhow, there wasn't any getting around that) and
seemed to feel none of the embarrassment which
Richard always felt acutely if he was seen with even
a little bit of a hard-up. He turned partly away,
though, in honor of Good Friday, and for the same
reason he and Richard glanced at each other with
even less candor than they would have at any other
time, and Richard the more uneasily crossed and un-
crossed his hands in front of himself. Only Hobe,
of any boy Richard knew, never concealed his own
body or his interest in another, and even now, Good
Friday seemed to mean nothing to him. He looked
at them, and watched them look at him, with a cool-
ness which seemed almost amused. He urinated a
few drops onto his belly and rubbed it in with the
palm of his hand, against cramps. He made no ges-
ture of covering himself and grabbed his testicles
with one hand only at the instant he grabbed his nose
with the other to leap with a spangling splash into
the water.

He bounced up with an incredulous strangling
yell and began a frenzied dogpaddle and both of
them knew the water must be even colder than they
had thought, and that there was no longer any

chance of holding back. Jimmy went in feet first;
Richard dove. The iron water distended enormously
just beneath him and for an instant, knowing the
brutal shock and the pain to which he had now in-
escapably committed himself, he felt the fatal exhil-
aration of a falling dream and had just time to dedicate within himself *for Thee!*, in a silent shout as
deafening bright as a smiting of cymbals; then plunged
into the smashing cold. Still crying *for Thee* within
his ringing head, he slanted his hands to dive as deep
as he could go and, though his eyes were open, could
see nothing of the steep sandstone along which his
hands guided him, but only the stifled effulgence of
light above. It was so much colder than he had been
able to imagine that in the first moment he had felt almost unconscious, but the diver's reflex had locked his
breath and now that he searched from ledge to ledge
downward along the much colder bottom there
sprang throughout his flesh such an ardent and serene
energy that he was aware of the entire surface of his
body as if it were fire, and every muscle seemed to
feel its own exact shape and weight, and he wished
that he need never come up and lay against the deepest trench of the bottom, his belly foundering in
ooze, his eyes shut, staying his hands on rocks. He
lifted his face free of the ooze and cautiously opened

his eyes; he could feel, more clearly than be sure
he saw, the light which enlarged above him. He
turned his head and looked up sidelong; there it was,
a pure, heavy slab of still light which by impercep-
tible degrees shaded downward into most deadly
darkness. His chest and his head began to knock, it
became harder with every pulse to hold onto the
rocks. O Lord let me suffer with Thee this day, he
prayed, his lungs about to burst; and took hold more
firmly. You got no right, his own voice silently told
him, you got no right. No right; but still he fought
off his need for air, filling his cheeks with the exhausted air from his lungs and taking it down again
in the smallest possible gulps. His head was beating
and ringing so fiercely that he could scarcely hear
the fragments of his own efforts to dedicate and to
reprove himself but blindly, with the last of his
strength, held himself down. Then he knew that he
had stayed down too long; too deep; he could not
possibly reach the air in time. Good. That's fine.
For Thee! he groaned. *No right! Get out!*, he
shouted silently. But even before he could command
it or fully decide to command it his body was work-
ing for him; his feet braced against a ledge, his knees
bent, and he leapt upward through the brightening
water with more strength than he had realized he had

left although the water seemed interminably tall above him and he knew still that he would never reach the surface in time and cried out to himself, *I didn't have the nerve!* and, *Anyhow I tried*, meaning at once that he had tried to stay down too long as an act of devotion and that he had tried to save himself from the deadliest of sins; and broke the surface in time, head back, gasping, feebly treading water, watching the streaming bruise-colored clamorous and silent whirling of the world and taking in air so deeply that his lungs felt as if they were tearing; and soon the world became stable and all of the coloring and discoloration cleared and stood up strongly through the top of the woods across the tracks and he could realize that except for the remote voices of the two boys and the still more remote voice of a bird the world itself was delicately silent and all the noise was within his own head and was rapidly dying: all that he saw still twitched with his pulse and out of the woods, beating like a heart, the sun stood up.

His teeth still ached at their roots and although he clenched them to keep them from chattering his chin trembled like a rabbit's nose and his breath came out shakily in many small pieces as of glass or ice. From its surface down to about his waist, the water seemed surprisingly warm, but from waist to knees it was grimly cold, and his stony feet trod a mortal bleakness of cold and dark to which he was thankfully sure now that he would never go down again. Yet except for his feet, which no longer seemed to belong to him, his body still blazed with pleasure in its existence, and it was no longer urgent and rigid but almost sleepy. He slid his slick hands along his ribs and his sides and found that in his sex he was as tightly shrunken as if he were a baby. I could have died, he realized almost casually. *Here I am!* his enchanted body sang. I could be dead right now, he reflected in sleepy awe. *Here I am!* Now that he had his breath and was quiet he no longer tried to control the rattling of his teeth but hung standing in the water, his head so turned from the others that they might not see the silent unexpected tears and, drowsily trying to make himself aware of the suffering to which at this moment Jesus was submitting Himself, crying for tenderness and thankful wonder, gazed steadily into the beating sun.

But staying still so long, coldness at length overcame him, and after swimming as fast as he could twice up and down the length of the quarry, he stumbled out.

He had all but forgotten them; they were already

drying themselves with their shirts. Hobe's body was purplish; Jimmy looked as if he had been caught in a blue net.

"What you trine to do?" Hobe asked. "Drownd yourself?"

"I was just swimming under water."

"I was damn near ready to dive in after you," Jimmy said, "when you come up."

"We began to think you was drownded," Hobe said.

"No, I was all right," Richard said. He reached for his shirt. *"Heyy!"* he shouted.

Steering, serenely, his sutured brow, the sum of those several thrusting curves which seemed not of themselves to exert strength but merely to drink and send backward through them the energies of the guiding head they guided, a snake more splendid than Richard had ever seen before was just achieving a sandstone ledge and the first heat of the risen sun. In every wheaten scale and in all his barbaric patterning he was new and clear as gems, so gallant and sporting against the dun, he dazzled, and seeing him, Richard was acutely aware how sensitive, proud and tired he must be in his whole body, for it was clear that he had just struggled out of his old skin and was with his first return of strength venturing his new one. His style and brightness, his princely elegance, the coldness of his eye and the knifelike coldness and sweetness of his continuously altering line, his cold pride in his new magnificence, were not at the first in the least dismayed, not even by Richard's shout; only the little tongue, to Richard's almost worshiping delight and awe, sped like a thready horn of smoke, the eye seemed to meet Richard's and become colder and still more haughty, and the vitality of his elegance advanced him still further along the stone: so that for a few seconds Richard saw perfected before him, royally dangerous and to be adored and to be feared, all that is alien in nature and in beauty: and stood becharmed. But as the others ran up, within an instant so swift that it was impossible to see just what transpired among those curves of liquid paroxysm, with a chilly rasping against stone which excited Richard as nothing he had ever heard before had excited him, drawing a stripe of coldness down his spine, the snake reversed direction and slipped rapidly between the ankles of briars and beneath fallen leaves, his brilliance a constant betrayal. The others were shouting and Jimmy shoved a stick under the snake and flipped him so expertly that for a couple of seconds he sailed on the air in a convulsion of escape, a fluid hieroglyph, and landed on open

rock in a humiliating flash of ivory belly before he
righted himself and with oily fleetness made once
more for the bushes. But now Hobe reared up a
rock so heavy he could lift it only clumsily, high
above his reeling head; and Richard, standing just behind him, felt himself reach towards the rock to pull
it backwards out of his hands. But even as his own
hand lifted forward he became aware of Jimmy's
astounded eye on him, and thus became aware of
what he was doing and caught himself, realizing that
they would never understand why he did it, that
they would be angry with him and rightly so and
might even be mad enough to jump on him; and becoming thus aware, became aware also that it was
not only his habit of gentleness to animals which
made him want to spare the snake, but something
new in him which he could not understand, about
which he was profoundly uneasy. These several
kinds of awareness came over him with terrible speed
and transfixed him into the slowness of a dream, so
that the fraction of a second froze the high rock,
the incredulous bystander, the bemused hand, and
seemed to last almost interminably, while he strove to
stay his hand and to set it free. But it was after all
only an instant, and before he could bring himself
out of this hesitation, Hobe brought the rock crash-

ing down against rock and against one arc of the
veering snake which, angled like a broken whip, continued uselessly to thrust energy through its ruptured
body, its eyes terrible, its tongue so busy that its
speed made the shadow of a blossom. Jimmy hurried
up with his stick and beat at its head but the head
was still alert to dodge under his blows. Richard felt
for a moment as if he had just finished retching.
Then he picked up a small rock and yelling *"Get out
of the way,"* squatted beside the snake and pounded
at its head. The head lashed about his fist like summer
lightning as he pounded and in the darkness of his
violence the question darted, over and over, *is he
poison? is he poison?* but he cared only for one thing,
to put as quick an end as he could to all this terrible,
ruined, futile writhing and unkillable defiance, and
at length he struck and dazed, and struck and missed,
and struck and broke the head which nevertheless
lifted senilely, the tongue flittering and the one remaining eye entering his own eye like a needle; and
again, and the head lay smashed and shifting among
its debris; and again, and it was flattened against the
stone, though still the body, even out beyond the
earlier wound, lashed, lay resting, trembled, lashed.

As he watched this trembling twitching, desper-
ately wishing that he could so crush the snake that it

would never move again, he realized that it would not die until sundown, and even as he realized this he heard Hobe say it and became aware, through something quiet in Hobe's voice and through Jimmy's shyness, that they respected him; that in putting his bare hand within range of that clever head and in killing so recklessly and with such brutality, he had lost their contempt and could belong among them if he wanted to. He looked coldly at his trembling hand: bloody at the knuckles and laced with slime, which seemed to itch and to burn as it dried, it still held the rock.

"Better warsh that stuff off," Hobe said. "Git in your blood: *boy!*"

He still squatted, looking at his hand and wondering. In their good opinion, and in the rugged feeling of the hand itself and its ferocious moisture, he began to feel that he had been brave in a way he had never been brave before and he wanted the hand to clear gradually and naturally, the way the smudge clears from the forehead on Ash Wednesday. He could not be sure, in its pristine skin, what kind of snake this was, and the head was wrecked beyond any hope of determining whether it had the coffin shape, or venomous fangs. But it was not a rattler, nor was it likely a copperhead, nor was it striped like a moccasin, so that he had to doubt whether, after all, it had been poisonous. If it had not been poisonous he had not been brave; and if it had not been poisonous he was sorry he had killed it or even been fool enough to yell so the others would see it and so automatically kill it, for he had for a long while been fascinated by snakes and had felt that the harmless ones ought to be let alone, as few people let them alone. He was aware that Hobe had spoken and that he had given no kind of answer, and this made him uneasy. He wanted very much to taste the slime; but they were watching. He turned up the rock and looked at it: the slime and breakage of the snake caught the whitening sunlight like mica. He slammed the rock into the middle of the water (just about where I dove in, he realized upon reflection) and clambered cautiously down to the edge and thrust his hand into the cold water and up to the elbow, beating quietly in the brilliant cold, and watched it in the water; the veins stood out on his forearm almost like a man. He decided that he would only submerge his hand, not wash it, no matter what Hobe advised. But Hobe said nothing.

They dressed thoughtfully and they had very little to say; now that they were on their way back there wasn't much to think about except the trouble

which waited for them. There would have been
trouble even if they had come straight back from
Chapel, for they had outstayed the watch they had
signed for by a long time. But they began to realize
now that it would not have been as bad as it was
bound to be now; maybe they'd even have been let
off. If they had gotten back to bed at any time before daylight it wouldn't have been as bad as it would
be now. If they had come in just while the sun was
rising it would have been bad but not as bad as this.
Now it was broad daylight and brighter every minute, and with every minute longer now that they
stayed away they were in for worse trouble. They
might be kept on bounds, they might have to pull
stumps or clean out the pit of the backhouse, they
might be whipped, they might even not be let go on
the Easter Monday picnic and they had planned to
go clear to Wet Cave which had never yet been fully
explored, and find new passages and if possible, a new
and secret entrance. There was no telling what, for
the worst of it was that they had gone against a strict
rule so conspicuously on Good Friday, and by taking
advantage of a religious event, and there was no way
of imagining how much more serious an offense this
might seem to priests than to people. The train came
down from Coal City and passed them while they

dressed, making a great deal of happy and vigorous noise, but it only sharpened their realization that by now everybody was up and around and that certain people would be looking for them and watching for them already, so that they hardly even had the heart to look up at the blank baggage car and the empty coach and to wave at the engineer who saluted them.

Richard didn't even look up as the train passed, nor had the thought of punishment very clearly entered his mind; all the while he dressed, he watched the snake. From the break on back it lay belly up and the pallor of the belly, and the different structure of the scales, so well designed for crawling, were quietly sickening to see. He tried to see all that he could see without looking at the annihilated head, but his eyes kept flicking back to where it lay, mashed almost like soft metal against the rock, almost as flat and ragged as the toadfrogs and pennies they used to put on the tracks in Knoxville, after the streetcar ran over them. The snake moved very weakly now, but strongly enough that Richard could not doubt it would keep moving, and blindly experiencing the agony of death, straight on through the morning and the Three Hour Service and on through the afternoon until, at last, as the top rim of the sun sank out of sight, the tip of the tail would give one last quaver and the snake would lie still forever.

"Well come on," he was startled to hear Hobe's voice at his shoulder. He turned to go.

"Aint you takin him?"

It had not occurred to Richard; now that it did, he certainly did not want him.

"No."

"Hell fahr, you kilt him didn you?"

"I don't want him."

Hobe and Jimmy glanced at each other. "Okay," Hobe said. He took the snake carefully by the tail. The break in the body held firm; the head pulled loose from the rock like adhesive tape. He snapped him like a whip; now most of the head was lost.

"He'll bust in the middle," Jimmy said.

"Hell I keer," Hobe said. But he did not snap the snake again. Half a snake wouldn't be worth showing.

On the far side of the track they fell into single file for the woods path, Hobe ahead, swinging the limpid snake at the new leaves, then Jimmy, then Richard. Without consulting or imitation, all three had put their shoes on when they dressed; they walked rather quickly, and they did not talk.

In refusing the snake, Richard realized, he had lost a considerable portion of their esteem, though not all of it. He was still regarded as the hero of this occasion and he knew he was still one of them in a

way he had never been before. He was still pleased
to have been accepted and still pleased with his own
courage, though he was sorry the snake had been
killed, and unhappy and uneasy whenever he caught
a glimpse of it ahead. He began to know how very
hungry he was and with his hunger he remembered
once again, with surprise and shame that he could
have forgotten, what Day this was. It must be on
past seven o'clock by now. He would not start
carrying the Cross until nine. By now He would
just be sitting on the stool or the bench in the gar-
rison room, probably sort of like a locker room,
while the soldiers paid Him no attention much but
just hogged their breakfasts and maybe threw cornbread at Him, no it wouldn't be cornbread; He just
sat there with nothing to eat or drink and some of
the worst things were already over by now; He sat
in the purple robe holding the reed and the blood
was drying on His back from the scourges and the
torn wounds were itching and the spit was drying on
His face (like my hand is drying), not just spit but
the nastiest kind of snot, too, if it happened here
they'd spit tobacco juice, and down through the
drying spit the blood ran from the Crown of Thorns;
how did they push those thorns down around His
forehead without hurting their hands? And here I

am, he thought, suddenly remembering the absolute-
ness of emotions during the moments just after he
woke up that morning. Here I am. He struck his
breastbone and tried to imagine how it would feel to
be scourged with a cat-o'-nine-tails with lead tips,
and to wear a crown of thorns. Busy with twisted
and uneven walking, he could not make it very clear
to himself. He closed his eyes and almost immediately stumbled on a root. Jesus falls for the first time,
he said to himself. God help me. God forgive me I
didn't mean it. He kept his eyes open and took care
how he walked.

The woods were full of ordinary sunlight now;
the colors were no longer strange and the deep per-
spectives were no longer mysterious, but pleasant and
casual. When they came to the clearing it was full of
simple light and the bird was no longer singing.
When they had come nearly to the other side of
this warm open silence Richard hurried back to the
tree on which he had left the locust shell, detached
it gently, and with great care, scarcely looking at it,
settled it into the breast-pocket of his shirt. They
were not far into the woods when he caught up. His
trotting and quick breathing, now that he slowed
again to a walk, made him aware once more of his
sharp hunger. It was going to be a long day without

food, without, if he could help it, even rinsing his mouth out with water. I'll help it, he told himself, imagining water in his mouth. I'll not do that, anyhow. He thought again of the thorns, and the spittle, and the patience and courage, and of his maculate hand. The least I can do, he told himself. The *least* I can do! The day lifted ahead of him very long and hard, a huge unshaded hill. The climbing of it would go on in the heavy sun without rest throughout this livelong day and forever so long as he might be alive and there at the top there was dying: His; his; so hard and so long. It won't be over till sundown, he said to himself. Such a terrible and cold heaviness distended in the pit of his stomach, and his knees became suddenly so weak, that for a few moments he had to lean against a tree, and found it difficult to breathe. He had never before known such heaviness or such cold, crushing sorrow. *"Forgive!"* he whispered, barely able to bring the word out: *"Forgive! O God forgive!"* But the cold and enormous heaviness only increased, and the sadness now seemed more than his soul could endure.

After a little, however, he regained sufficient strength in his knees, and walked again, by now a good way behind the others. But the heaviness stayed, so that he felt as if he were carrying an all but impossible weight in the middle of his body.

By now they could see the first of the buildings through the lightleaved woods; and now the whole of the School stood up before them and the two boys ahead walked more slowly, wondering what lie, if any, might lighten their trouble. But they could not think of any that would do and when Richard overtook them, lingering unhappily at the stile, they were so far beyond hope that they didn't even bother to ask him whether he had any ideas.

Now that he was with them again, the heaviness was somewhat less severe, and he began to wonder what had made him so deeply weak and unhappy, and what kind of trouble they would be in for; now he could clearly foresee Father Whitman's hard sleepless eyes in his first look at them as they would come up from the woods, their hair spiky with incriminating wetness; and much as he dreaded in advance the punishment, which would be a whipping for sure, he told himself, he dreaded even more the first meeting with these eyes, and the first words that would be spoken, though he suspected that these would be tempered to the day. He heard Jimmy say to Hobe that he better get rid of that snake, and he thought that he sure better; and he was neither surprised nor particularly troubled when, a few moments later, Hobe slung the snake in among the hogs. He stood with the other children at the fence and

watched with interest while two of the hogs, with
snarling squeals, scuffled over the snake, tore it apart
at its middle wound and, while the two portions still
tingled in the muck, gobbled them down. It occurred
to him, with a lancing quailing of horror and pity,
that the snake was still alive, and would stay alive in
their bellies, however chewed, and mangled, and dif-
fused by acids, until the end of the day; but now, remembering the head, he told himself that the snake
was so far gone by now that he must be a way beyond really feeling anything, ever any more (the
phrase jumped at him): (Who had said that? His
mother. "Daddy was terribly hurt so God has taken
him up to Heaven to be with Him and he won't
come back to us ever any more.") "Ever any more,"
he heard his quiet voice repeat within him; and within
the next moment he ceased to think of the snake with
much pain. When the boys turned from the sty he
followed them towards the Main Building carrying,
step by step with less difficulty, the diminishing
weight in his soul and body, his right hand hanging
with a feeling of subtle enlargement at his thigh, his
left hand sustaining, in exquisite protectiveness, the
bodiless shell which rested against his heart.

Date Due